CONTENTS

G000061375

0860 10 50 50
www.mapstudio.co.za

Production Manager: John Loubser
Cartographic Manager: Christine Flemington
Cartographer: Malcolm Palmer
Research: Abbygail Botha
Graphic Design & Index: Malcolm Palmer

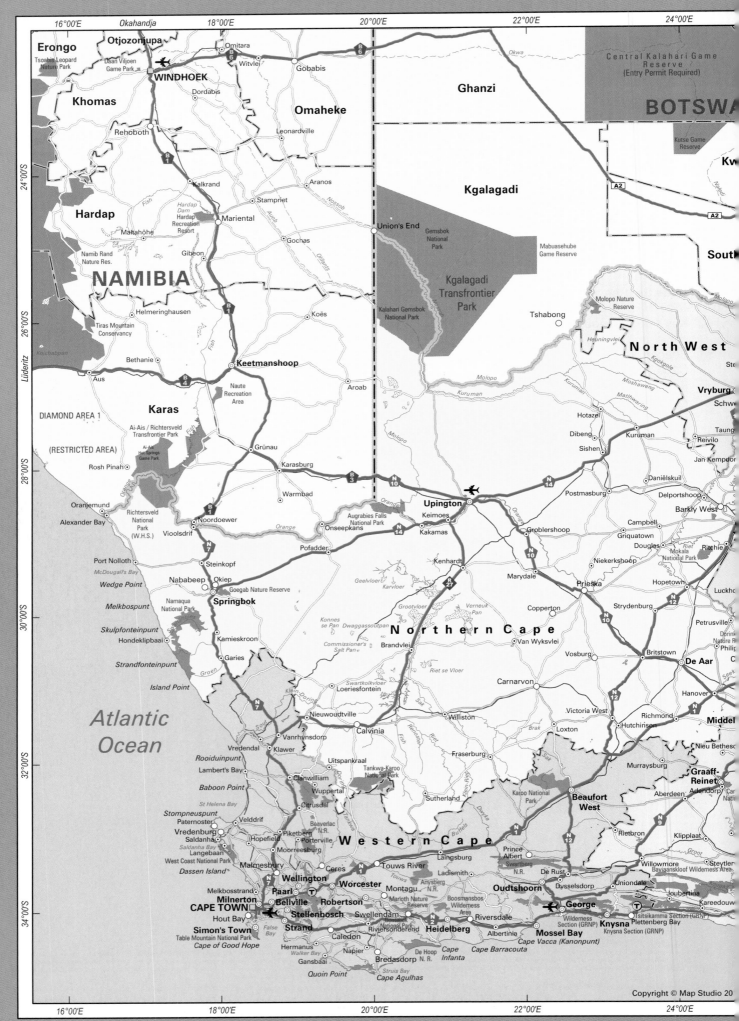

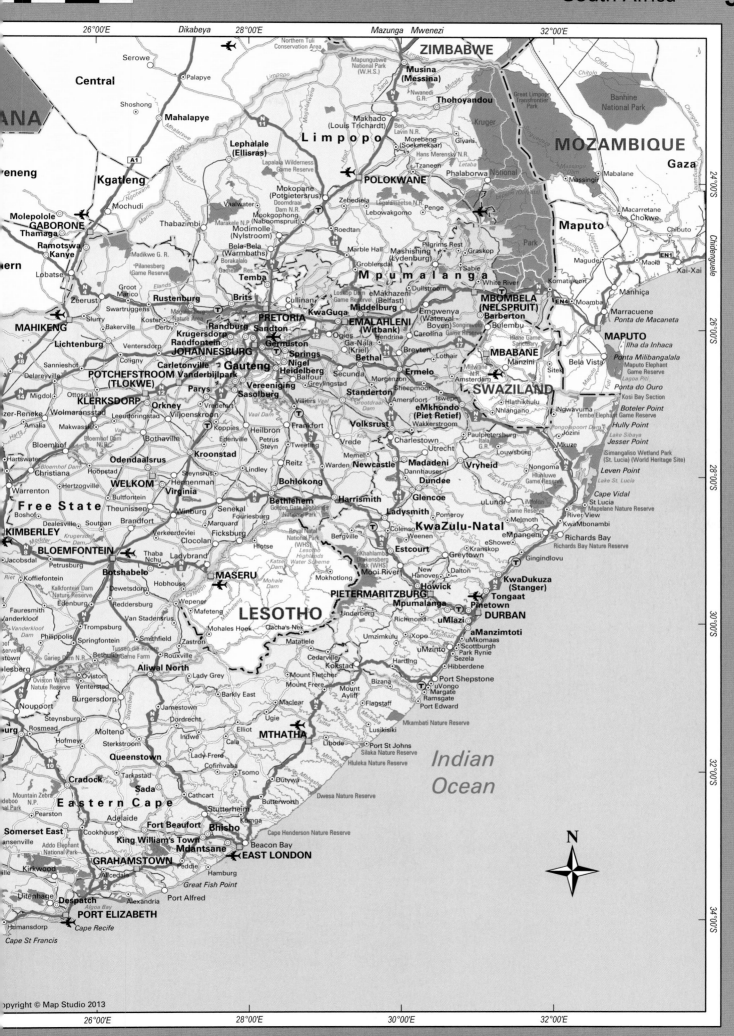

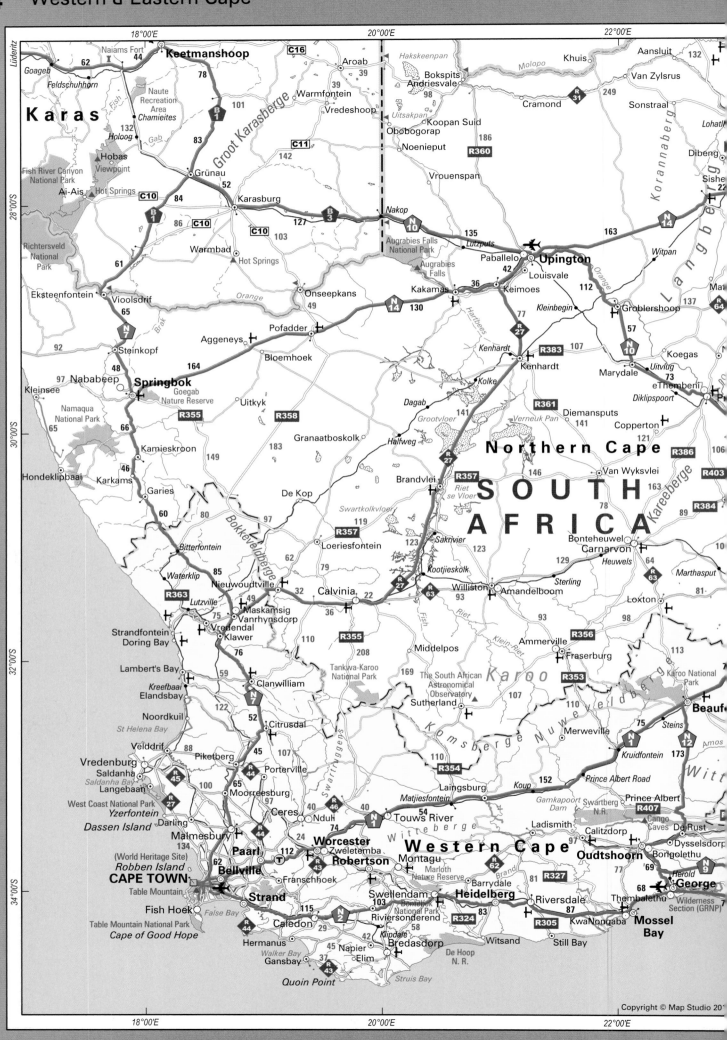

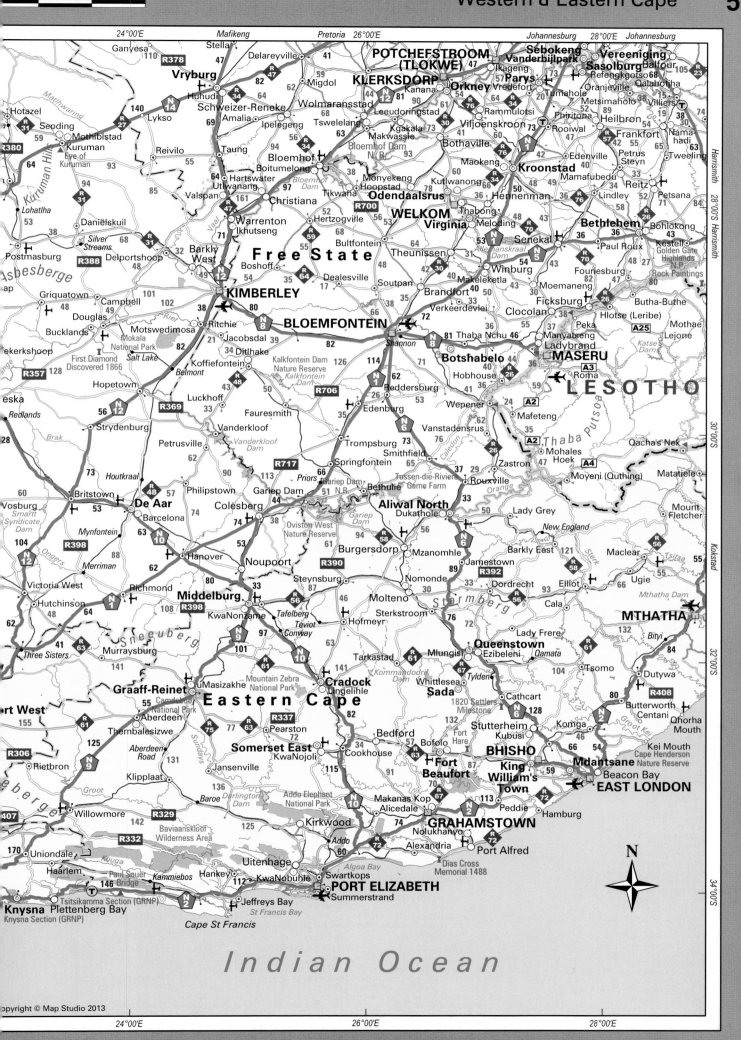

SOUTH AFRICA USEFUL NUMBERS
SA National Parks (Pretoria) 012 428 9111
General Directory Enquiries 1023
International Enquiries 10903
Telkom Information Centre 012 311 3911
Police 10111
Ambulance 10177
AA Breakdown 0800 111 998
Cellular Emergencies
Cell-C 084 140
MTN 083 173
Vodacom 082 111
Money Matters
ABSA 0800 111 155
American Express 011 710 4750
Diners Club 011 358 8400
Europ Assistance 011 991 8000 / 9000
First National Bank 0800 110 132
Mastercard International 0800 990 418
Nedbank 0800 110 929
Rennies Foreign Exchange (Thomas Cook) 0860 11 11 77
Standard Bank 0800 020 600
Thomas Cook Rennies 0800 998 175
Visa International 0800 990 475
COUNTRYWIDE AIRPORT INFORMATION
OR Tambo International Airport 011 921 6262
Bloemfontein 051 407 2240
Cape Town International Airport 021 937 1200
Central Reservations 011 978 1111
Durban International Airport 031 451 6666
George 044 876 9310
Mthatha Airport 047 536 0023
SA Express 011 978 5569
SAA Reservations 0861 585 852
Weatherline 082 162
CAR HIRE / RENTALS
Avis Rent-a-Car 086 102 1111
Hertz Reservations 0861 600 136
National Car Rentals 0800 01 13 23
Budget Rent-a-Car 0861 016 622
TRANSPORT
Automobile Association 0800 111 997
Transnet Freight Rail 086 000 8888
Blue Train 021 449 2672
Metrorail 0800 65 64 63
BUS SERVICES
Baz Bus 021 439 2323
Greyhound 021 418 4326/083 915 9000
Intercape 0861 28 72 87/021 380 4400
Translux 0861 589 282

WESTERN CAPE TOURISM INFORMATION
Cape Town
·Cape Town Holocaust Centre 021 462 5553
·Cape Town International Convention Centre 021 410 5000
·Castle Of Good Hope 021 787 1249
·District Six Museum 021 466 7200
·Mount Nelson Hotel 021 483 1000
·Planetarium 021 481 3900
·Radisson Blu Hotel, Waterfront 021 441 3000
·Robben Island Museum 021 413 4220/1
·SA Museum 021 481 3800
·South African National Gallery 021 467 4660
·St George's Cathedral 021 424 7360
·Table Mountain Aerial Cableway 021 424 8181
·Cape Town Tourism (Cableway) 021 422 1075
·Two Oceans Aquarium 021 418 3823
·Cape Town Tourism (V&A Waterfront) 021 408 7600
·Two Oceans Aquarium 021 418 3823
·V&A Waterfront 021 408 7600
The Cape Peninsula & Northern Suburbs
·Blaauwberg Tourism Office 021 521 1080
·Cape of Good Hope Gate (Table Mountain National Park) 021 780 9526
·Table Mountain National Park 021 701 8692
·Cape Point Ostrich Farm 021 780 9294
·Grass Roots 021 706 1006
·Ilios Travel 021 697 4056
·Two Oceans Restaurant 021 780 9200
·Citysightseeing Cape Town 021 511 6000
Camps Bay
·Bay Hotel 021 438 4444/ 021 437 9701 (Bookings)
·Blues Restaurant 021 438 2040
·Theatre on the Bay 021 438 3301
Constantia
·Buitenverwachting 021 794 5191
·Constantia Uitsig 021 794 6500
·Constantia Village 021 794 5065
·Groot Constantia 021 794 5128
·Klein Constantia 021 794 5188
·Jonkershuis Restaurant 021 794 6255
·Kirstenbosch Botanical Garden 021 762 0687
·Steenberg Estate 021 713 2211
Durbanville & Tygerberg Region
·Altydgedacht 021 976 1295
·Bloemendal Wines 021 976 2682
·Diemersdal Wines 021 976 3361
·Durbanville Hills Wines 021 558 1300
·GrandWest Casino 021 505 7777
·Meerendal Estate 021 975 1655
·N1 City Shopping Centre 021 595 1170
·Nitida Estate 021 976 1467
·Tygerberg Nature Reserve 021 913 5695
·Willowbridge 021 915 4080
·Tyger Valley Shopping Centre 021 914 1822
·Tygerberg Zoo 021 884 4494
Fish Hoek
·Simon's Town 021 786 8440
Hout Bay
·Chapman's Peak Hotel 021 790 1036

·Mariner's Wharf 021 790 1100
·Hout Bay Visitor Information Centre 021 791 8380
·World of Birds 021 790 2730
Kalk Bay
·Cape to Cuba 021 788 1566
·Olympia Cafe 021 788 6396
Kommetjie
·Imhoff Farm 021 783 4545
·Noordhoek 021 789 2812
Melkbosstrand / Milnerton
·Canal Walk Shopping Centre 021 529 9699/8
·Koeberg Nuclear Power Station Visitors Centre 021 550 4667
·Cape Town Tourism (Canal Walk) 021 555 3100
·Ratanga Junction 0861 200 300
Muizenberg
·Muizenberg 021 787 9140,
Newlands
·Cavendish Square Shopping Centre 021 657 5620
·Kirstenbosch National Botanical Garden 021 799 8783
·South African Breweries 021 658 7511
Noordhoek
·Noordhoek 021 789 2812
Simon's Town
·Boulders Beach (Table Mountain National Park) 021 786 2329
·Simon's Town 021 786 8440,
·Simon's Town Museum 021 786 3046
·South African Naval Base 021 787 3911
·Warrior Toy Museum 021 786 1395
The Winelands Region
·Somerset West 021 840 1400
·Winelands Tourist Information 0861 265 263
Gordon's Bay, Strand & Somerset West
·Somerset West 021 840 1400
·Cape Town Tourism (Strand) 021 853 1688
·Cape Town Tourism (Gordon's Bay) 021 856 1444
·Monkey Town 021 858 1060
·Somerset Mall Shopping Centre 021 852 7114
·Vergelegen 021 847 1334
Franschhoek Winelands Region
·Boschendal Estate 021 870 4200
·Haute Cabrière 021 876 8500
·Franschhoek Tourism Bureau 021 876 3603
·Huguenot Museum 021 876 2532
·La Motte 021 876 3114
·La Petite Ferme 021 876 3016
·Môreson Estate 021 876 3055,3692
Paarl Winelands Region
·Afrikaans Language Museum 021 872 3441
·Butterfly World 021 875 5628
·La Bonheur Crocodile Farm 021 863 1142
·Fairview Wine Estate 021 863 2450
·KWV (HO & Wine Emporium) 021 807 3007
·Nederburg 021 862 3104
·Paarl Museum 021 872 2651
·Paarl Tourism Bureau 021 872 0860
Stellenbosch Winelands Region
·Bergkelder 021 809 8025
·Delheim Wine Estate 021 888 4600
·Historical Walks 021 883 9633
·Morgenhof 021 889 5510
·Oom Samie se Winkel 021 887 0797
·Spier 021 8091100
·Stellenbosch Information Office 021 883 3584
·Stellenbosch Museum 021 887 2902
·Stellenbosch Wine Route 021 886 4310
·Van Rhyn Brandy Cellars 021 881 3875
Wellington Winelands Region
·Hottentots-Holland Nature Reserve 028 841 4826
·Bokomo Foods 021 864 8690
·Wellington Museum 021 873 4710
·Wellington Wine Route & Tourism 021 873 4604
West Coast, Overberg, Karoo And Garden Route Region
·Breede Valley Tourism 023 348 2795
·Central Karoo Regional Tourism Office 023 449 1000
·The Garden Route Klein Karoo Regional Tourism Organization 044 873 6314
·Hex Valley Tourism 023 356 2041
·Overberg Tourism 028 425 1157
·West Coast Regional Tourism 022 433 8505
Arniston
·Arniston Hotel 028 445 9000
·Tourist Info 028 424 2584
Barrydale
·Tourist Info 028 572 1572
Beaufort West
·Karoo National Park 023 415 2828
·Beaufort West Tourism 023 415 1488
Bredasdorp
·De Hoop Nature Reserve 028 542 1253
·Tourist Info 028 424 2584
·Bredasdorp Museum 028 424 1240
Caledon
·Caledon Hotel 028 214 5100
·Tourist Info 028 212 3282
Ceres
·The Fruit Route 023 316 1287
·Kagga Kamma Nature Reserve 021 872 4343
·Matroosberg Reserve 023 312 2282
·Togryers Museum (Transport Riders' Museum) 023 312 2045
·Tourist Info 023 316 1287
Citrusdal
·Tourist Info 022 921 3210
Clanwilliam
·Cederberg Wines 027 482 2827
·Cederberg Wilderness Area & Nature Reserve 027 482 2812
·Die Kunshuis Art Gallery 027 482 1940
·Rooibos Ltd – Tea & Natural Products 027 482 2155
·Tourist Info 027 482 2024
Darling
·Evita se Perron 022 492 2831/2851
·Rondeberg Nature Reserve 022 492 3435

·Tourist Info 022 492 3361
·Wild Flower Line 022 492 3361, 083 910 1028
Dwarskersbos
·Tourist Info 022 783 1821
Eland's Bay
·Crayfish permits at the Post Office 022 972 1700
·Tourist Info 022 972 1640
Elgin & Grabouw
·Elgin Valley Tourism Bureau 021 848 9838
·Elgin Apple Museum 021 848 9060
·Paul Cluver Amphitheatre 021 844 0605
Elim
·Tourist Info 028 482 1806, 084 974 8731
George
·George Museum 044 873 5343
·Fancourt Hotel and Country Club 044 804 0010
·Outeniqua Choo-Tjoe 044 801 8288
·Outeniqua Nature Reserve 044 870 8323/5
·Outeniqua Railway Museum 044 801 8288
·Tourist Info 044 801 9103
Greyton
·Greyton Lodge 028 254 9876/9800
·Greyton Nature Reserve 028 254 9414
·Tourist Info 028 254 9414/9564
Hermanus
·Bouchard Finlayson Vineyards 028 312 3515
·Hamilton Russell Vineyards 028 312 3595
·Hermanus Whale Hotline 028 312 2629
·Old Harbour Museum 028 312 1475
·Tourist Info 028 312 2629
Hopefield
·Tourist Info 022 723 1720
Jacobsbaai
·Tourist Info 022 714 2088
Kleinplasie
·Kleinplasie Living Open Air Museum 023 342 2225/6
Kleinmond
·Tourist Info 028 271 5657
Knysna
·Featherbed Nature Reserve 044 382 1693
·Knysna Forest 044 382 5466
·Knysna Oyster Co. 044 382 6941/2
·Knysna Quays Waterfront 044 382 0955
·Mitchell's Brewery 044 382 4685
·Nature's Valley 044 531 6700
·Outeniqua Choo-Tjoe 044 801 8288
·Tourist Info 044 382 5510
Laingsburg
·Tourist Info 023 551 1868
Lambert's Bay
·Tourist Info 027 432 1000
Langebaan
·Club Mykonos 022 707 7000
·Die Strandloper 022 772 2490
·Postberg Nature Reserve 022 772 2144
·Tourist Info 022 772 1515
·West Coast Fossil Park 022 766 1606
·West Coast National Park 022 772 2144
·Wild Flower line 022 772 1515
Malmesbury
·Sasko Grain (Bokomo Mills) 022 482 7272
·Malmesbury Museum 022 482 2332
·Swartland Wine Route 022 487 1133
·Tourist Info 022 487 1133
Matjiesfontein
·Lord Milner Hotel 023 561 3011
McGregor
·Tourist Info 023 625 1671
·Vrolijkheid Nature Reserve 023 625 1621
Montagu
·Montagu Hot Mineral Springs 023 614 1050
·Montagu Museum 023 614 1950
·Tourist Info 023 614 2471
Mossel Bay
·Tourist Info 044 691 2202
Oudtshoorn
·CP Nel Museum 044 272 7306
·Cango Caves 044 272 7410
·Cango Ostrich Farm 044 272 4623
·Cango Wildlife Ranch 044 272 5593
·Swartberg Nature Reserve and Pass 044 203 6325
·Tourist Info 044 279 2532
Paternoster
·Cape Columbine Lighthouse 022 752 2705
·Columbine Nature Reserve 022 752 2718
·Tourist Info 022 752 2323
Piketberg
·Historic Watermill 022 913 1947
·Piketberg Museum 022 913 1126
·Tourist Info 022 913 2063
·Winkelshoek Wine Cellar 022 913 1092
Plettenberg Bay
·Goukamma Nature Reserve 044 383 0042
·Nature Conservation & Reserves 044 802 5310
·Tourist Info 044 533 4065
Porterville
·Groot Winterhoek Nature Reserve 022 931 2088
·Tourist Info 022 931 3732
Port Owen
·Port Owen Marina 022 783 1144
·Tourist Info 022 783 1821
Prince Albert
·Tourist Info 023 541 1366
Robertson
·Dassieshoek Nature Reserve 023 615 8000/8038
·De Wetshof Wine Cellars 023 615 1853
·Graham Beck 023 626 1214
·Robertson Museum 023 626 3681
·Robertson Wine Valley 023 626 3167
·Soekershof (World's largest maze) 023 626 4134
·Tourist Info 023 626 4437

Saldanha
•SAS Saldanha Nature Reserve 022 702 3523
•Tourist Info 022 714 2088
Sedgefield
•Goukamma Nature Reserve 044 383 0042
•Tourist Info 044 343 2658
St Helena
•Tourist Info 022 715 1142
•Vasco da Gama Nautical Museum 022 742 1906/1199
Still Bay / Stilbaai
•Tourist Info 028 754 2602
Swellendam
•Bontebok National Park 028 514 2735
•Wildebraam Liqueur Farm 028 514 3132
•The Drostdy Museum 028 514 1138
•Marloth Nature Reserve 028 514 1410
•Tourist Info 028 514 8580
Tulbagh
•Tourist Info 023 230 1348/1375
Vanrhynsdorp
•Kokerboom Succulent Nursery 027 219 1062
•Latsky Radio Museum 027 219 1032
•Gifberg Holiday Resort 027 219 1555
•Tourist Info 027 219 1552
Velddrif
•Tourist Info 022 783 1821
Vredenburg
•Vredenburg Golf Course 022 715 3003
•Tourist Info 022 715 1142
Vredendal
•Matzikama Eco Park 027 213 3794
•Spuitdrift Wine Cellar 027 213 3086
•Tourist Info 027 201 3376
•Vredendal Co-op 027 213 1080
Wilderness
•George/Wilderness Tourism 044 877 0045
Witsand
•Tourist Info 028 537 1010
Worcester
•Karoo National Botanic Garden 023 347 0785
•Tourist Info 023 348 2795
Wupperthal
•Tourist Info 027 492 3410
Yzerfontein
•Tourist Info 022 451 2366

EASTERN CAPE TOURISM INFORMATION

9 EASTERN CAPE TOURIST ROUTES TO EXPLORE
Tsitsikamma 042 280 3561
Kouga Region 042 293 2923
Sundays River Valley Route 042 230 0066
Sunshine Coast Tourism 046 648 2418
Karoo Heartland 049 892 4248
Frontier Country 046 622 3241
Amatola Mountains Escape 043 642 2571
Friendly N6 051 633 3567
Wild Coast 047 531 5290 / 2

EASTERN CAPE TOURIST BOARDS AND BODIES
•Eastern Cape Tourism Board 043 701 9600
•Eastern Cape Tourism (Mthatha) 047 531 5290 / 2
•Tourist Information Centre Port Elizabeth Nelson Mandela Bay Tourism 041 585 8884
•ECTOUR 041 507 7912
•South African Tourism (H/O) 011 895 3000

EASTERN CAPE TOURIST OFFICES
•Aberdeen Municipality 049 846 0014
•Adelaide (Nxube Municipality) 046 684 0034 / 0177
•Alexandria (Ndlambe Tourism) 046 624 1235, 648 2418
•Alice 046 645 7454
•Alicedale Municipality 042 231 1013
•Aliwal North 051 633 3567
•Amatole District Municipality 043 701 4000
•Barkly East Community Tourism 045 971 0724
•Bathurst-Ndlambe Tourism Port Alfred Unit 046 624 1235
•Bedford Tourism 046 685 0076 / 0187
•Buffalo City 043 721 1346
•Burgersdorp Community Tourism Office 051 653 0595
•Cathcart Municipality 045 843 1022
•Cradock Tourism 048 801 5000
•Cookhouse Municipality 042 247 1166
•Info Somerset East 042 243 1333
•Despatch Municipality 041 933 1111
•Info Despatch Library 041 994 1616
•Dordrecht Tourism 045 943 1642
•Elliot Municipality 045 931 1011, 082 701 7754
•Fort Beaufort-Kat River 046 645 1555 (Library)
•Graaff-Reinet Publicity 049 892 4248
•Grahamstown (Makana Tourism) 046 622 3241
•Hankey Tourism 042 284 0543
•Herschel Tourism Sterkspruit 051 611 0031 / 0065
•Haga-Haga, Morgan Bay, Kei Mouth 043 841 1645 / 1062
•Hofmeyr Municipality 048 885 0097 / 082 777 4482
•Hogsback Tourism 045 962 1130, 043 722 5054
•Humansdorp Tourism 042 295 1361
•Jamestown Municipality 051 641 0641
•Jansenville Municipality 049 836 0021
•Kareedouw Municipality 042 288 0303
•Jeffreys Bay Tourism 042 293 2923 / 2588
•Kei Bridge Information 043 831 2004
•Kei District (OR Tambo District Council) 047 501 6400
•Keiskammahoek Municipality 040 658 0028
•Kenton-Bushmans Tourism Office 046 648 2418
•King William's Town (Buffalo City Tourism Office) 043 721 1346
•Lady Frere Municipality 047 878 0020
•Lady Grey Community Tourism Office 051 603 0176
•Langkloof Tourism 042 273 1065 / 1516, 082 498 1045
•Maclear / Ugie Tourism 045 933 1335 / 7 / 932 1550
•Middelburg Karoo Tourism Bureau 049 842 1337
•Molteno Municipality 045 967 0021
•Nelson Mandela Bay Tourism (Port Elizabeth) 041 582 2575
•Ngcobo 047 548 1221
•Nieu-Bethesda Municipality 049 841 1623 / 42 / 59
•Patensie (Kodomo Tourism Office) 042 283 7912 / 13 / 14
•Tolbos (Gamtoos Tourism Office) 042 238 0437
•Port Alfred Tourism 046 624 1235
•Port Elizabeth (see Nelson Mandela Bay Tourism)
•Port St Francis (see St Francis Bay Tourism) 042 294 0076
•Port St Johns Tourism 047 564 1187, 1207/8
•Queenstown Information Office 045 839 2265, 073 424 9912
•Rhodes Tourism 045 974 9305
•St Francis Bay Tourism 042 294 0076
•Steynsburg Municipality 048 884 0034
•Steytlerville Municipality 049 835 0022 / 0153
•Somerset East Bluecrane Tourism Route 042 243 6448
•Stutterheim (Amahlathi Municipality) 043 683 1100
•Sundays River - Greater Addo 042 230 0066 / 0562
•Tarkastad Community Tourism Office 045 846 0324
•Tsitsikamma Tourism Information 042 280 3561, 281 1849
•Uitenhage Municipality 041 994 1408
•Mthatha Wild Coast Tourism 047 531 5290 / 2
•Venterstad Municipality 051 654 0224
•Wild Coast Reservations 043 743 6181
•Willowmore Municipality 044 923 1004

EASTERN CAPE ADVENTURES & ACTIVITIES
Biking
•Graaff-Reinet 049 892 4248
•Hogsback Mountain Bike Trail 043 722 5054, 082 200 3489
•Nieu-Bethesda Hire a Bike 049 841 1642
•Port Elizabeth Logmore Forest Mountain Bike Trail & Baakens River Mountain Bike Trail 041 583 2030, 082 774 8771
•Rhodes Mountain Biking 045 974 9305 / 9290
Bird Watching
•Barkly East Bird Club 045 971 0016, 082 929 1512
•Gonubie Nature Reserve 043 740 4000, 741 2212
•Graaff-Reinet Bird Club 049 891 0353, 083 560 7367
•Jeffreys Bay Tourism (Kabeljous Nature Reserve,Seekoei River Nature Reserve, the Noorsekloof & Paradise Beach 042 293 2923 / 2 0339
Dolphin & Whale Watching
•Port St Johns 047 564 1121, 082 550 5437
Entertainment in Port Elizabeth
•The Boardwalk Casino & Entertainment World 041 507 7777
Fishing
•East London Deep Sea Fishing 043 735 2604
•Port St Johns Fly Fishing 083 775 2082
•Rhodes Wild Trout Association 045 974 9290
•Wild Cat Fishing Charter 082 654 9629
Haunted Walks
•Port Elizabeth 041 583 2584
Hiking
•Port St Johns 082 507 2256
Horse trails
•Guided Horse Trails & Game drives 042 233 8600
•St Francis Bay Oyster Bay Lodge 042 297 0150
Hunting
•Eastern Cape Tourism Board 043 701 9600
•Eastern Cape & Karoo Safaris 083 655 5597
Mountain Climbing
•Nieu-Bethesda 049 841 1635
•Port Elizabeth Mountain Club of South Africa 041 365 5543
Sand Boarding
•Boardroom 041 586 2276
•Go Experiences 041 583 3451

Eastern Cape Tour Operators
•Amadiba Adventures 039 305 6356
•Amahlati Excursions 046 622 4517, 083 631 4800
•Amanzi River Rafters, Cradock 048 881 4433
•Amanzi Tours 041 364 0169
•Bay Tours, Port Elizabeth 041 584 0056
•Beyond Adventures, East London 043 743 5778
•Birdwatching & Eco Tours 041 466 5698, 073 252 4111
•Bukani Travel & Tours 041 464 7812, 083 657 2666
•Calabash Tours, Port Elizabeth 041 585 6162
•Charter Flights, East London Air 043 736 1663
•Dtours, Tarkastad 045 848 0152
•Friendly City Tours (Port Elizabeth) 041 585 1801
•Frontier Country Connections, Grahamstown 046 622 8054
•Golf n Game, Port Elizabeth 041 373 3092, 082 930 0768
•Helicopter Charter and Training, 041 507 7343
•Imonti Tours, East London 083 487 8975
•Indudumo Ventures, Port Elizabeth 041 378 1418
•Jarandi Tours & Safaris, Port Elizabeth 082 295 9521
•Graaff-Reinet 049 892 3978
•Karoo Experience Tours, Middelburg 049 842 1790
•Kyalami Tours, Port Elizabeth 082 485 2759
•Kelly's Tours, Port Elizabeth 046 648 2545, 082 450 7771
•Kwanti Safaris, Port Elizabeth 082 551 5752
•Let's Go Tours, Port Alfred 046 624 1866
•Lynx Tours, Jeffreys Bay 042 296 0594 / 2563
•Maximum Exposure Adventure, Port Alfred 046 624 4432
•Pembury Tours, Port Elizabeth 041 581 2581 / 2403
•Saunter Tours, Port Elizabeth 041 366 1315
•Shumba Safaris, Hankey 082 576 2642
•Shield Tours, Port Elizabeth 041 453 5513
•Speirs Tours, King William's Town 043 642 1747
•Southern Cross Safaris, Cradock 048 886 0606 / 66
•Springbok Atlas, Port Elizabeth 041 581 2555
•Stormsriver Adventures 042 281 1836
•Sunshine Express, Jeffreys Bay 082 449 5735
•Swartkei Safaris, Tarkastad 040 845 1100
•Tanaqua Tours, Port Elizabeth 083 270 9924
•Turaco Tours, Port Elizabeth 041 379 1406, 082 784 3242
•Turquoise Horizen, East London 043 748 6128
•Tsitsikamma Canopy Tours 042 281 1836
•Pure African Tours, Hankey 042 284 0516, 072 891 0222
•Umzantsi Africa, Port Elizabeth 082 361 9733, 082 822 4717
•YQK Tours, Alice 082 400 3911

18-Hole Golf Courses In The Eastern Cape
•Aliwal North 051 634 1887
•East London 043 735 1356
•Fish River 040 676 1002
•Grahamstown 046 622 2106
•Humewood 041 583 2137
•Port Elizabeth 041 374 3140
•Royal Port Alfred 046 624 4796
•St Francis Bay 042 294 0467
•Uitenhage 041 966 1868
•Walmer Country Club 041 581 4211
•Wedgewood Park 041 372 1212

Eastern Cape 9-Hole Golf Courses
•Adelaide 046 684 0489
•Alexandria 046 653 0207
•Barkly East 045 971 0742
•Bedford 046 685 0123
•Butterworth 047 491 4370
•Cathcart 045 843 1041
•Cradock 048 881 4548
•Dirk Fourie Trust 042 285 0321
•Dordrecht 082 596 5822
•Elliot 045 931 1094
•Fort Beaufort 046 645 1959
•Gonubie 043 740 5645
•Graaff-Reinet 049 893 0286
•Hankey 042 284 0335
•Humansdorp (Swartenbos Golf Course) 042 291 0529 / 0569
•Indwe 082 924 8234, 045 952 1123
•Jansenville 049 834 9034 / 6 9076
•Jeffreys Bay 042 293 2532
•Kei Mouth 043 841 1083
•Kirkwood 042 230 0452
•Komga 043 831 1069
•Lady Grey 051 603 0006
•Middelburg 049 842 4456
•Molteno 045 967 0251
•Shark River 041 581 6188
•Somerset East 042 243 3993
•Steynsburg 048 884 0311
•Steytlerville 049 835 0155
•Stutterheim 043 683 1508
•Walmer 041 581 1613
•Willowmore 044 923 1261 / 044 923 1177

Eastern Cape Hiking Trails
•Alexandria Hiking Trail, Alexandria 042 233 8600
•Amadiba Adventures, Wild Coast 50km 039 305 6455
•Amatola Hiking Trail 043 642 2571 / 4148
•Dolphin Trail,Tsitsikamma 17km 042 281 1607
•Kariega Game Reserve Trail 8-10km 043 636 7904 / 0263
•Lammergeier, Lady Grey 051 603 1114
•Mkambathi Nature Reserve, Flagstaff 039 727 3273 / 253 8079
•Otter Trail, Tsitsikamma 42km 042 281 1607
•Settlers Hiking Trail, Port Alfred 046 625 0660
•Sunshine Coast Trails, Port Alfred 046 624 5295
•Strandloper Hiking Trail, Kei Mouth 043 841 1046
•Transkaroo Hiking Trail, Middelburg 049 843 1506
•Wild Coast Meander 55km, Wild Coast Amble 56km
•Wild Coast Pondo Walk 46km 043 743 6181
•Wild Coast Trails (Amadiba Adventures) 039 305 6455 / 7
•Woodcliffe Cave, Maclear 39km 011 412 1888, 656 0606

Eastern Cape Short Hiking Trails
•Addo National Park Trail 042 233 8600
•Baviaanskloof Hiking Trails 043 742 4450
•Bloukrans Walking Tours 042 281 1458
•Cape St Francis Nature Reserve 042 298 0054
•Cradock Bushman Trail, Mountain Zebra Trail 048 881 2427
•Graaff-Reinet Karoo Trail 049 892 3453
•Grahamstown Area, Valley of the Ancient Voices 4 hour Guided Walking Trail 046 622 3241 / 8511
•Groendal Hiking Trail 041 992 5418
•Humansdorp Boskloof Nature Reserve 042 295 1361
•Hogsback Walking Trails, Amatola Guesthouse 045 962 1059
•Hogsback Trails 045 962 1302 / 1
•Nieu-Bethesda, Ganora Guest Farm 049 841 1302
•Nukakamma Canoe Trail, Sundays River Mouth 041 468 0238
•Oldenburgia Hiking Trail 046 622 3241
•Port Elizabeth, Gamtoos River Mouth 041 585 8884,
•Sundays River Valley Hiking Trails & Horse Riding, Addo Elephant National Park 042 233 8600
•Storms River Trail 042 281 1607
•Two Rivers Hiking Trail, Grahamstown 046 622 3241

Eastern Cape National Parks And Reserves
•Addo Elephant National Park 042 233 8600
•Amakhala Game Reserve 042 235 1608
•Baviaanskloof Nature Reserve 043 742 4450
•Burchell Game Reserve 042 231 1302, 083 270 4606
•Commando Drift, Tarkastad, Friendly N6 043 742 4450
•Double Drift Game Reserve, Frontier Country 040 653 8010
•Dwesa / Cwebe Reserves, Wild Coast 043 742 4450
•Hluleka Nature Reserve, Wild Coast 043 742 4450
•Inkwenkwezi Private Game Reserve 043 734 3234
•Kamala Game Reserve 042 243 3507, 083 235 9927 / 28
•Kariega Game Reserve, Kenton-on-Sea 046 636 7904
•Kwandwe Private Game Reserve 046 603 3400, 011 809 4300
•Kwantu Private Game Reserve, Greater Addo Paterson 084 500 0345, 083 500 0344
•Lalibela Game Reserve, Addo 041 581 8170
•Lombardini Reserve, Jeffreys Bay 042 293 2073
•Mkhambathi Nature Reserve, Wild Coast 043 742 4450
•Misty Mountain Reserve, Tsitsikamma 042 280 3699
•Molweni Private Game Reserve 046 684 0261
•Mountain Zebra National Park, Cradock, Karoo Heartland 048 881 2427, 012 428 9111
•Mpofu Game Reserve, Fort Beaufort, 043 742 4450
•Mpongo Private Game Reserve 043 709 5038
•Schotia Safaris Private Game Reserve 042 235 1436
•Seaview Game and Lion Park, Port Elizabeth 041 378 1702
•Shamwari Private Game Reserve 042 203 1111
•Silaka Reserve, Wild Coast 043 742 4450, 041 407 1000
•Timbila Game Reserve 044 923 1188
•Garden Route National Park 042 281 1607, 042 280 3561
•Tarkastad 040 845 1112, 043 742 4450
•Umgamanzi Game Lodge & Safaris041 368 1244

EASTERN CAPE ACCOMMODATION

Addo
- Darlington Lake Lodge 042 243 3673
- Gorah Elephant Camp 044 532 7818
- Stellenhof Country House 042 233 2423

Alexandria Bushmans River Mouth
- Heritage Lodge Guest House 046 653 0024
- Kikuyu Lodge 046 653 9039
- Sandon On Sea 046 654 0217, 083 321 9848

Amatola Mountains Escape
- Mpofu Nature Reserve 040 864 9450, 043 742 4450

Beacon Bay
- Blue Lagoon Hotel 043 748 4821

Bathurst
- Protea Hotel Bathurst 046 625 0833
- Pig & Whistle Hotel 046 625 0673

Bedford
- Cavers Country House 046 685 0619

Cintsa / Wild Coast
- Cintsa Lodge 043 738 5146
- Crawfords Cabins 043 738 5000
- Inkwenkwezi Private Game Reserve 043 734 3234

Cradock
- Die Tuishuis 048 881 1322
- Heritage House 048 881 3210
- Mountain Zebra Park 048 881 2427, 012 428 9111
- Oude Pastorie Lodge 048 881 3011
- Palm House 048 881 4229
- Southern Cross Safaris 048 886 0606

East London
- Blue Lagoon Hotel 043 748 4821
- Chelsea Square 043 743 0397
- Bluewaters Lodge 043 740 2019
- Devereux Lodge 043 726 9459
- Dolphin View Lodge 043 702 8600
- King David Premier Hotel 043 722 3174
- Lagoon Valley Resort 043 736 9753
- Meander Inn 043 726 2310
- Quarry Lake Inn 043 707 5400
- Quintetta Guest Farm 043 748 4729

Elliot
- Merino Hotel 045 931 2987
- Mountain Shadows Hotel 045 931 2233
- Rose Garden 045 931 1158, 082 771 8947
- Tulloch 043 740 0470
- Intaba Lodge 045 931 1402

Friendly N6 Region
- Tsolwana Nature Reserve 043 742 4450

Frontier Country
- Double Drift 043 742 4450, 040 653 8010
- Kwandwe Game Reserve 046 603 3400, 011 809 4300
- Molweni Private Game Reserve 046 684 0261

Gonubie
- Boardwalk Beach House 043 740 2290
- Gonubie Hotel 043 740 4010
- Gonubie Point Guest House 043 740 4279, 082 824 1419
- Seaspray 043 740 4234, 082 920 3189
- The Crowned Crane 043 740 3505, 082 568 2274
- The Gonubie Sun B&B 043 740 4507
- The White House B&B 043 740 0344

Graaff-Reinet
- Avondrust Guest House 049 892 3566
- Drostdy Hotel 049 892 2161
- Eenzaamheid Holiday Farm 049 845 9011
- Langfontein Guest Farm 049 845 9021, 082 655 6900

Grahamstown
- Albany Hotel Group 046 622 2324
- Graham Hotel 046 622 2324
- Lantern Hill B&B 046 622 8782
- Oak Lodge Hotel 046 622 9123
- Settlers Hill Cottages 046 622 9720
- The Cock House 046 636 1287 / 95, 082 820 5592

Greater Addo Paterson
- Amakhala 042 235 1608
- Dreamers Armadale B&B 042 230 0908
- Highfields B&B 042 235 1269, 082 773 0722
- Lalibela Game Reserve 041 581 8170
- Sandflats B&B and Self-Catering 042 235 1012
- Shamwari 042 203 1111

Hankey
- Schumba Safari Lodge 042 284 0828

Hogsback
- Granny Mouse House 045 962 1259
- Kings Lodge 045 962 1024
- Lowestoff Country Lodge 045 843 1716
- May Lodge Country Cottages 045 962 1016
- The Edge 045 962 1159

Jeffreys Bay
- Al Kynaston 042 296 1845
- Beach Cabanas Holiday Units 042 293 2820
- Beach Music 042 293 2291
- Costa Cara 042 293 4160
- Diaz 15 042 293 1779
- Dirkie's Dream 042 293 3909
- Greystone Guest House 042 296 0616
- Lazee Bay B&B 042 296 2090
- Sandkasteel 042 293 1585
- Savoy Hotel 042 293 1106
- Seester Strandhuis 042 293 4397
- Supertubes Guest House 042 293 2957
- The Haven 042 296 1926
- The White House 042 293 3116

Kenton-On-Sea
- Amblewood 046 648 2957
- Burke's Nest 046 648 1894, 082 577 2142
- Carriage House 046 648 1129, 082 928 4660
- Hillcrest House B&B 046 648 2961
- Kariega Game Reserve 046 636 7904
- Lime Tree House 046 648 1226
- The Milking Parlour 046 622 8395
- Wings 046 648 1834

- Woodlands Country Cottages 046 648 2867
- Woodside B&B 046 648 1802, 082 219 0235

King William's Town
- Dreamers Guest House 043 642 3012

Langkloof
- Louterwater Landgoed 042 272 1724
- The Kraaltjie Guest House 082 498 1045

Middelburg
- Caro Chalets 049 842 2910
- Carlton Heights 049 842 2017
- Karoo Country Inn 049 842 1126

Patensie
- Baviaanskloof Nature Reserve 043 742 4450
- Gamtoos B&B 082 655 6236
- Gonjah Chalet 042 283 0596
- Orchard View Guest House 042 283 0248, 084 240 7057

Port Alfred
- Fish River Sun 040 676 1101
- Medolino Resort 046 624 1651
- Oribi Haven 046 648 2043, 084 477 1166
- The Halyards Hotel 046 604 3300
- The Residency 046 624 5382
- Villa Majestic 046 624 2857

Port Elizabeth
- Africa Beach B&B 041 583 5833
- Apron Strings 041 366 2320 / 1217
- Beacon Lodge 041 583 5061
- Beach Hotel 041 583 2161
- Beachwalk B&B 041 583 3594
- Brookes Hill Suites 041 584 0444
- Bishops Inn 041 585 6828
- Cape Flame Guest House 041 583 3666
- Edward Protea Hotel 041 586 2056
- Humewood Hotel 041 585 8961
- Ikhayalam Lodge 041 582 5098
- Kasama Lodge 041 583 4579
- King's Tide Boutique Hotel 041 583 6023
- Margate Place Guest House 041 583 5799
- Park Place 041 585 5062
- Paxton Hotel 041 585 9655
- Summerstrand Hotel 041 583 3131
- Summer House B&B 041 583 4854
- Sylvesters Guest House 041 373 1889
- The Kelwey Hotel 041 584 0638
- Victorian Villa Guest Manor 041 373 5359
- Wilma's Guest House 041 583 1527

Rhodes
- Rhodes Hotel 045 974 9305
- Tiffindell Ski Resort 011 679 2994

Somerset East
- Golden Valley Hotel 042 247 1155
- Lantern Square B&B 042 243 2566, 082 831 0713
- Noah's Art 042 243 1925
- Somerset House 042 243 1819 / 3935

St Francis Bay
- Beach Break 042 298 0054
- Cape St Francis Resort 042 298 0054
- Lyngenfjord House 042 298 0444
- Milkwood Country Cottages 042 294 1007
- Port St Francis Estate 042 294 1223
- Samaki Beach Lodge 042 294 0270
- Sandriver Lodge 042 294 1052
- Waterways B&B 042 294 0282

Stutterheim
- The Manderson 043 683 2322

Sundays River Valley & Addo Region
- Addo Elephant National Park 042 233 8600
- Chrislin African Lodge 042 233 0022
- Cosmos Cuisine 042 234 0323
- Good Hope Country House 042 234 0357
- Gorah Elephant Camp 044 532 7818, 042 235 1123
- Homestead B&B 042 233 0354
- Hopefield Country House 042 233 0333
- Stellenhof Country House 042 233 2423
- Valleyview B&B 042 233 0349, 082 411 0434
- Zuurberg Mountain Inn 042 233 8300
- Carrickmoor Guest Farm 045 846 9252
- Lesley's B&B 045 846 0481

Tsitsikamma Region
- Misty Mountain Reserve 042 280 3699
- The Fennery 042 280 3588
- Tsitsikamma Lodge 042 280 3802
- Tsitsikamma National Park 042 281 1607
- Tsitsikamma On Sea 042 280 3697

Wild Coast Region
- Coffee Shack 047 575 2048
- Country Lodge 047 532 5730
- Cremorne Estate 047 564 1110
- Haga Haga Resort 043 841 1670
- Hluleka Nature Reserve 043 742 4450
- Kob Inn 047 499 0011
- Lily Lodge 047 564 1229
- Mbotyi River Lodge 039 253 8822
- Mitford Lodge 043 841 1510
- Mkhambathi Nature Reserve 043 742 4450
- Morgan Bay Hotel 043 841 1062
- Ocean View Hotel 047 575 2005
- Seagulls Beach Hotel 047 498 0044
- Silaka Nature Reserve 043 742 4450
- The Estuary Country Hotel Port Edward 039 311 2675
- Trennery's Hotel 047 498 0004
- Umngazi River Bungalows 047 564 1115/6/7
- Wavecrest Resort Hotel 047 498 0022
- Wild Coast Sun 011 780 7800

Willowmore
- Timbila Game Reserve 044 923 1188

EASTERN CAPE CARAVAN AND CAMPING
- Addo Elephant National Park 042 233 8600

Aliwal North
- Aliwal Spa 051 633 2951

Bushmans River Mouth

- Boesmans Caravan Park 046 648 3584

Cannon Rocks
- Cannon Rocks Holiday Resort 046 654 0043 / 0095

Cape St Francis
- Holiday Resort 042 298 0054

Cintsa East
- Cintsa Holiday Resort & Caravan Park 043 738 5064 / 5544
- Arendsnes 043 734 3015

Cradock
- Commando Drift Nature Reserve & Dam 048 881 3925

East London
- Glen Eden Resort 043 734 3033
- Club Arena Riverside Resort 043 734 3055
- Palm Springs 043 781 1901 / 1990
- Gonubie Gonubie Caravan Park 043 740 5937

Graaff-Reinet
- Urquart Caravan Park 049 892 2136, 049 891 0427

Grahamstown
- Grahamstown Caravan Park 046 622 3241

Hamburg
- Hamburg Caravan Park 040 678 0042

Jeffreys Bay
- Jeffreys Bay Caravan Park and Campsite 042 200 2241

Port Alfred
- Beyond Adventure Campsite 046 624 3159, 043 743 5778
- Medolino Caravan Park 046 624 1651 / 2514
- Riverside Caravan Park 046 624 2230 / 2702
- Willows Caravan Park 046 624 5201 / 3666

Port Elizabeth
- Pine Lodge Holiday Resort 041 583 4004 / 3839
- Willows Holiday Resort 041 366 1717 / 1878
- Van Stadens River Mouth 041 776 1059 / 1077

Somerset East
- Besterhoek Caravan Park 042 243 1333 / 1548

Stutterheim
- Kologha Camping Site 043 683 2474

Tsitsikamma Region
- Storms River Mouth 042 281 1607, 012 428 9111
- Khoisan Caravan Park 042 281 1450 / 1457

Wild Coast Region
- Central Reservations 047 531 1191
- Cremorne Estate 047 564 1113
- Morgan Bay Caravan Park 043 841 1062
- Wild Coast Holidays 043 743 6181
- Fish River Sun Hotel and Country Club Resort 040 676 1101

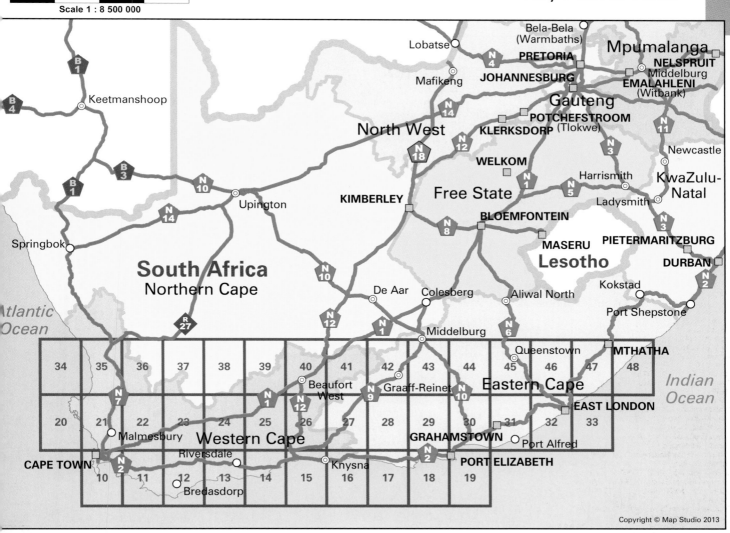

Scale 1 : 8 500 000

South Africa — Northern Cape, Western Cape, Free State, North West, Eastern Cape, Gauteng, Mpumalanga, KwaZulu-Natal, Lesotho

Places: Lobatse, Bela-Bela (Warmbaths), PRETORIA, JOHANNESBURG, Mafikeng, Keetmanshoop, NELSPRUIT, Middelburg, EMALAHLENI (Witbank), POTCHEFSTROOM, KLERKSDORP (Tlokwe), WELKOM, Newcastle, Harrismith, Ladysmith, KIMBERLEY, BLOEMFONTEIN, MASERU, PIETERMARITZBURG, DURBAN, Upington, Springbok, De Aar, Colesberg, Aliwal North, Kokstad, Port Shepstone, Queenstown, MTHATHA, Beaufort West, Graaff-Reinet, Middelburg, EAST LONDON, Malmesbury, Riversdale, GRAHAMSTOWN, Port Alfred, CAPE TOWN, Bredasdorp, Knysna, PORT ELIZABETH

Atlantic Ocean, Indian Ocean

Grid numbers: 34 35 36 37 38 39 40 41 42 43 44 45 46 47 48 / 20 21 22 23 24 25 26 27 28 29 30 31 32 33 / 10 11 12 13 14 15 16 17 18 19

Copyright © Map Studio 2013

Legend to Atlas Section

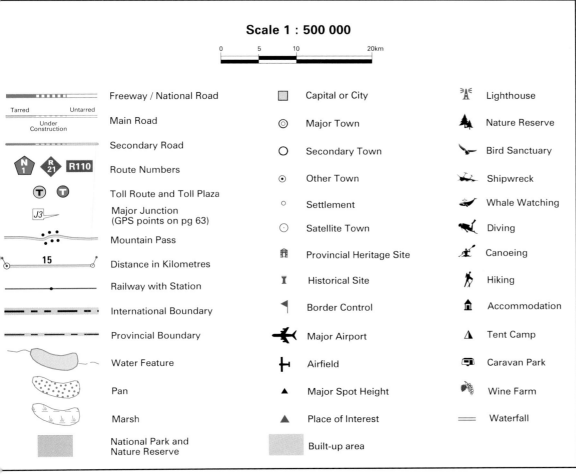

Scale 1 : 500 000

	Freeway / National Road (Tarred / Untarred / Under Construction)
	Main Road
	Secondary Road
N1 R21 R110	Route Numbers
T T	Toll Route and Toll Plaza
J3	Major Junction (GPS points on pg 63)
	Mountain Pass
15	Distance in Kilometres
	Railway with Station
	International Boundary
	Provincial Boundary
	Water Feature
	Pan
	Marsh
	National Park and Nature Reserve

▫	Capital or City
◎	Major Town
○	Secondary Town
⊙	Other Town
○	Settlement
⊙	Satellite Town
🏛	Provincial Heritage Site
	Historical Site
	Border Control
✈	Major Airport
	Airfield
▲	Major Spot Height
▲	Place of Interest
	Built-up area

	Lighthouse
🌲	Nature Reserve
	Bird Sanctuary
	Shipwreck
	Whale Watching
	Diving
	Canoeing
	Hiking
	Accommodation
△	Tent Camp
	Caravan Park
	Wine Farm
	Waterfall

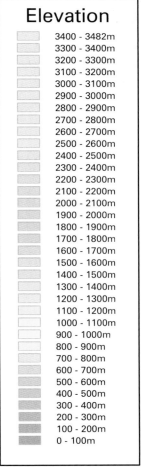

Elevation

	3400 - 3482m
	3300 - 3400m
	3200 - 3300m
	3100 - 3200m
	3000 - 3100m
	2900 - 3000m
	2800 - 2900m
	2700 - 2800m
	2600 - 2700m
	2500 - 2600m
	2400 - 2500m
	2300 - 2400m
	2200 - 2300m
	2100 - 2200m
	2000 - 2100m
	1900 - 2000m
	1800 - 1900m
	1700 - 1800m
	1600 - 1700m
	1500 - 1600m
	1400 - 1500m
	1300 - 1400m
	1200 - 1300m
	1100 - 1200m
	1000 - 1100m
	900 - 1000m
	800 - 900m
	700 - 800m
	600 - 700m
	500 - 600m
	400 - 500m
	300 - 400m
	200 - 300m
	100 - 200m
	0 - 100m

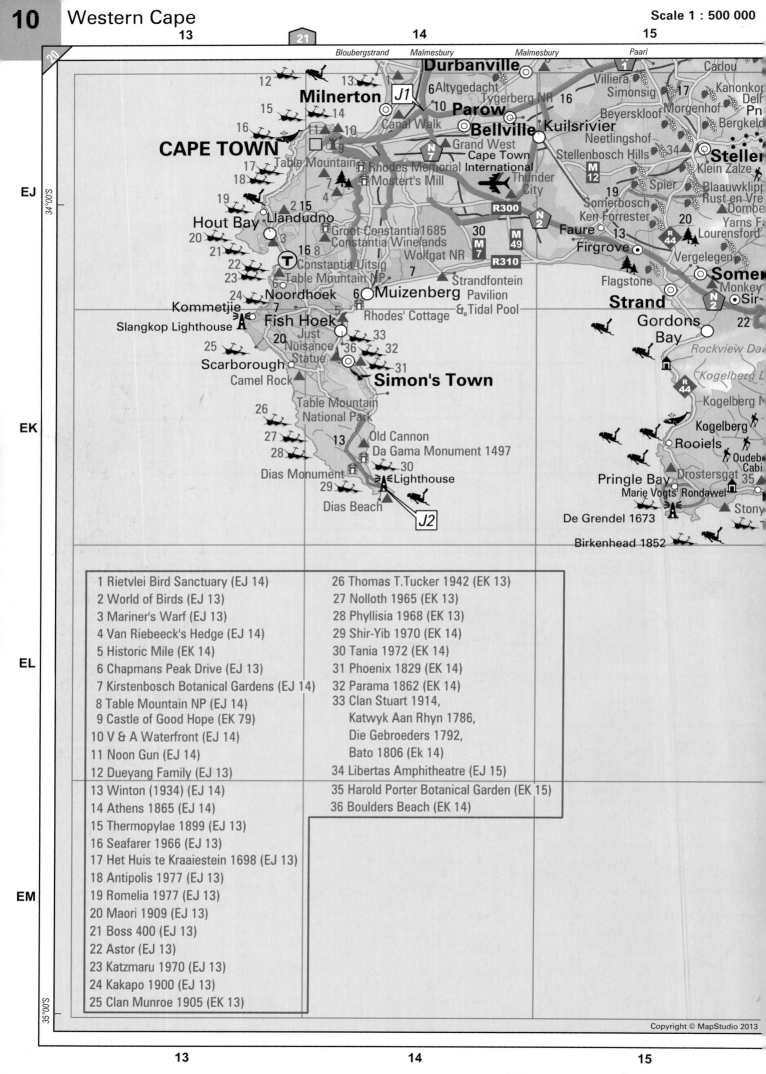

20
21
13 14 15

Blouberstrand Malmesbury Malmesbury Paarl

Durbanville
Carlou

Milnerton J1
6 Altygedacht
Tygerberg NR 16 Villiera Simonsig 17 Kanonkop Delf
10 Parow
Morgenhof Pn
Bellville Kuilsrivier Beyerskloof Bergkeld
Canal Walk Neetlingshof
CAPE TOWN Grand West Stellenbosch Hills 34 Steller
Cape Town International Klein Zalze
Rhodes Memorial Spier Blaauwklipp
Table Mountain Mostert's Mill Thunder City 19 Rust en Vre
7 R300 Somerbosch Dombe
4 N2 Ken Forrester 20 Yarns F
2 15 Faure 13 Lourensford
Hout Bay Llandudno 30 M49 Firgrove Vergelegen
3 Groot Constantia 1685 M7
Constantia Winelands R310 Somer
16 8 Wolfgat NR Flagstone
Constantia Uitsig 7 Monkey
T Table Mountain NP Strandfontein Strand Sir-
Noordhoek 6 Muizenberg Pavilion Gordons
Kommetjie 7 & Tidal Pool Bay Rockview Da
Slangkop Lighthouse 5 Rhodes' Cottage
Fish Hoek Kogelberg
25 20 Just 33
Scarborough Nuisance 36 32 R44 Kogelberg N
Camel Rock Statue 31 Kogelberg
Simon's Town Rooiels
Table Mountain Oudeb
26 National Park Old Cannon Cabi
27 13 Da Gama Monument 1497 Drostersgat 35
28 30 Pringle Bay
Dias Monument Lighthouse Marie Vogts Rondawel Stony
29 De Grendel 1673
Dias Beach J2 Birkenhead 1852

34°00'S EJ
EK
EL
EM
35°00'S

1 Rietvlei Bird Sanctuary (EJ 14)	26 Thomas T.Tucker 1942 (EK 13)
2 World of Birds (EJ 13)	27 Nolloth 1965 (EK 13)
3 Mariner's Warf (EJ 13)	28 Phyllisia 1968 (EK 13)
4 Van Riebeeck's Hedge (EJ 14)	29 Shir-Yib 1970 (EK 14)
5 Historic Mile (EK 14)	30 Tania 1972 (EK 14)
6 Chapmans Peak Drive (EJ 13)	31 Phoenix 1829 (EK 14)
7 Kirstenbosch Botanical Gardens (EJ 14)	32 Parama 1862 (EK 14)
8 Table Mountain NP (EJ 14)	33 Clan Stuart 1914,
9 Castle of Good Hope (EK 79)	Katwyk Aan Rhyn 1786,
10 V & A Waterfront (EJ 14)	Die Gebroeders 1792,
11 Noon Gun (EJ 14)	Bato 1806 (Ek 14)
12 Dueyang Family (EJ 13)	34 Libertas Amphitheatre (EJ 15)
13 Winton (1934) (EJ 14)	35 Harold Porter Botanical Garden (EK 15)
14 Athens 1865 (EJ 14)	36 Boulders Beach (EK 14)
15 Thermopylae 1899 (EJ 13)	
16 Seafarer 1966 (EJ 13)	
17 Het Huis te Kraaiestein 1698 (EJ 13)	
18 Antipolis 1977 (EJ 13)	
19 Romelia 1977 (EJ 13)	
20 Maori 1909 (EJ 13)	
21 Boss 400 (EJ 13)	
22 Astor (EJ 13)	
23 Katzmaru 1970 (EJ 13)	
24 Kakapo 1900 (EJ 13)	
25 Clan Munroe 1905 (EK 13)	

2.5 5   10   15   20 Kilometers

16 **17** **22** **18**

Paarl 19°00'E   Worcester   23

Vrede en Lust

Stettynskloof Dam

Silwerstrand Holiday Resort

Ormarins   48

                                        Stettyn Trail   Amathuhzi Reserve
Bellingham Groendal   (4x4)
Kylemore Boschendal Franschhoek   Hammanshof   Agterkliphoogte
         Le Franschhoek Huguenot Monument   Doornrivier - 1790
shoogte Hotel   EJ
osch   Franschhoek Pass   Boerbok
ottentots-Hollands NR   2   Theewaters NR   Bo-Radyn   Whipstock Farm
                            29   (1777)   Riviersonderend NR
                                 R45   Villiersdorp   Hester   Greyton-McGregor
                    Boesmanskloof   Dorothea   Boesmanskloof
                    Rest Camp   R45   Centre
         1590m   Boland   9   Sailing Club   Old Moravian Mission   Historic Street
    Triple Jump   R45   Genadendal Bell Tower
    Falls   Theewaterskloof   Bereaville Greyton
et West Landdroskop Rest Camp   Country Club   Bainbrecht Bridge
         R321   R406
wry's Pass   Nuweberg Dam   Theewaterskloof   R406
         Eikenhof Dam   Dam   Dwarskloof
    Grabouw   30   R
    Paul Cluver Elgin Houwhoek 33   N2   36
 J3 Houwhoek Houwhoek Inn   Boontjieskraal NR   27
romvlei   Beumont   3   Wildflower Garden   Krige
    Highlands Houhoek Pass 21 Botrivier   14 J5   EK
Palmiet   9   Swar   Caledon   Drayton
         J4 10   Caledon 29 Jongensklip
    Office   R320   Casino
                  Jeans Hill Hut Arabella Country Club   & Spa   Oukraal R326
                       Wild Horses De Bos 41 R320 Shaws Pass   J6
    13   Sonesta Dam   Bouchard Finlayson   26
tty's Bay Kleinmond Resort Hamilton   Fernkloof NR   White Water   Mountain
oint Penguin Colony 11   Russell   Kogelberg Lodge Akkedisberg Fairfield
e Meridian 1821 Hawston Onrus   Birkenhead Pass Arch Rock Balancing Rock
         Hermanus   Lake View Chalets Brewery 23   Leopard Cave
                   Kwaaiwater   River Cruises 35   Salmons Dam NR
         Shell Corner Beach   Art & Craft Stanford Suikerboshoek
                       Whale Rock Route 22 J7   Waterfall
                       Walker Bay   R43   Papiesvlei
                       Die Grou Duine   Moravian Church
         Shark Cage Diving Duiwelsgat Greetbos PR   & Clock
                            Cliff Path Byeneskrans Baardskeerdersbos
                   Gansbaai   Boesmans   41   Elim
                                                              Nieuwedam Farm B&B
         HMS Birkenhead 1852 Boat Trips to Heidenhof   Wolvengat Gallery
                            Dyer Island   Bosluis
                            Walker Bay NR Pearly Pearly Beach Resort
                                       Beach   37
                                                                                EL
                            Buffelsjag Holiday Resort
                                       Hynd 1947   Die Dam
                                       Swona 1947   Die Dam Holiday
                                                              Resort
                                                                                12
1 Car Museum (EJ 16)
2 Jan Joubertsgat Bridge (1823) (EJ 16)

Atlantic Ocean

19°00'E

34°00'S

35°00'S

EM

16 **17** **18**

19   23   20   21

22

Robertson   Robertson 20°00'E   Robertson/Montagu   Montagu

Voogdsrivier
Beck
Bree
Resort

Major's Hill
Springfield
Ashton

Rogmanskloof Pass

Montagu Mtn Reserve
Cheese Factory

Poortjieskloof
Dam

Sanbona
Nature Reserve
Joubert
Tradauw

McGregor
Meander
Van
Loveren
14
Nooitgedacht
61
Groot

Historic
Buildings
Vrolijkheid NR
Rooikat
Wolvendrift &
Goedverwacht
Nordale
Rietrivier
Proteavallei
Proteavallei
Klipbok Trail
4x4

McGregor
McGregor
Groot
Van Zylshof
Cheese Factory
Bonnievale
Bonnievale
46
Marloth Nature Reserve
Wolfkloof Hut
Goedgeloof Hut
Boskloof Hut
Forest Station

Boesmanskloof
Traverse
Langverwacht
& Janéza
Weltevrede
Merwespont
Church Square
Rheenendal Mill
Soothey
Arms

EJ
34°00'S
Gregor
kloof
Low Bridge, Drift
Jubilee
Bree
Drostdy
Swellendam
Scenic
Drive
11
Buffe

Boesman's

Stormsvlei
J8
Riviersonderend
Kam'Bati 4x4
Bontebok
National Park

11
Caledon
Lindeshof
Photo
Museum
N2
24
J9
13
Lang
Elsie's Kraal

Riviersonderend
20

10

27
Langkuil
Napkei

EK
Caledon
Caledon
Protem
R319
58
Malgas Hotel
N.G. Church 1856

Hansiesrivier
Gold Mine
Klipdale
Kykoedie
J11
Wydgeleë
De Hoo
Po

ld
R316
R317
Potberg Enviromental
Education Centre

Feeshuis
NG Church
Sout
Buchu Bushcamp
Tierhoek
Picnic Spot
Koppie-Alleen
Hut

Napier
16
De Hoopvlei
Bird Watching
De Hoop
Vaalkran
Hut

Kakebeenwa (Ox Wagon)
Monument
Giant Milkwood Tree
(Provincial Heritage Site)
Vlei Trails
Die Mond
Koppie
Alleen
Whale
Trail

Church
ck
J10
Church Hall and Manse
Bredasdorp

EL
Historic Watermill
Elim Mission Station
11
Heuningberg
NR
Shipwreck Museum
Bontebok Fence Monument
Kaasiesbaai
Fishing Village
Skipskop

Kars
R319
Die Herberg Resort
24
Clan McGregor 1902

23
26
Waenhuiskrans
Fisherman's Cottages

Voëlvlei
Soetendalsvlei
Sterna Trail Forest Station
Tsaba-Tsaba NR
Waenhuiskrans NR
Waenhuiskrans & Arniston
Waenhuiskrans Cave

11
Bird
Watching
De Mond
De Mond NR
Maggie (1843)
Arniston 1815

24
Fisherman's Cottages
Hotagterklip

m
Agulhas NP
L'Agulhas Caravan
Park
1
2
3
Struisbaai
Oriental Pioneer 1974

ay
L'Agulhas
Lighthouses
Museum
Lighthouse 1848

EM

1 Thatch Roof Church (EM 19)
2 Harbour Lights (EM 20)
3 Struisbaai Caravan Park (EM 20)

35°00'S
20°00'E

19   20   21

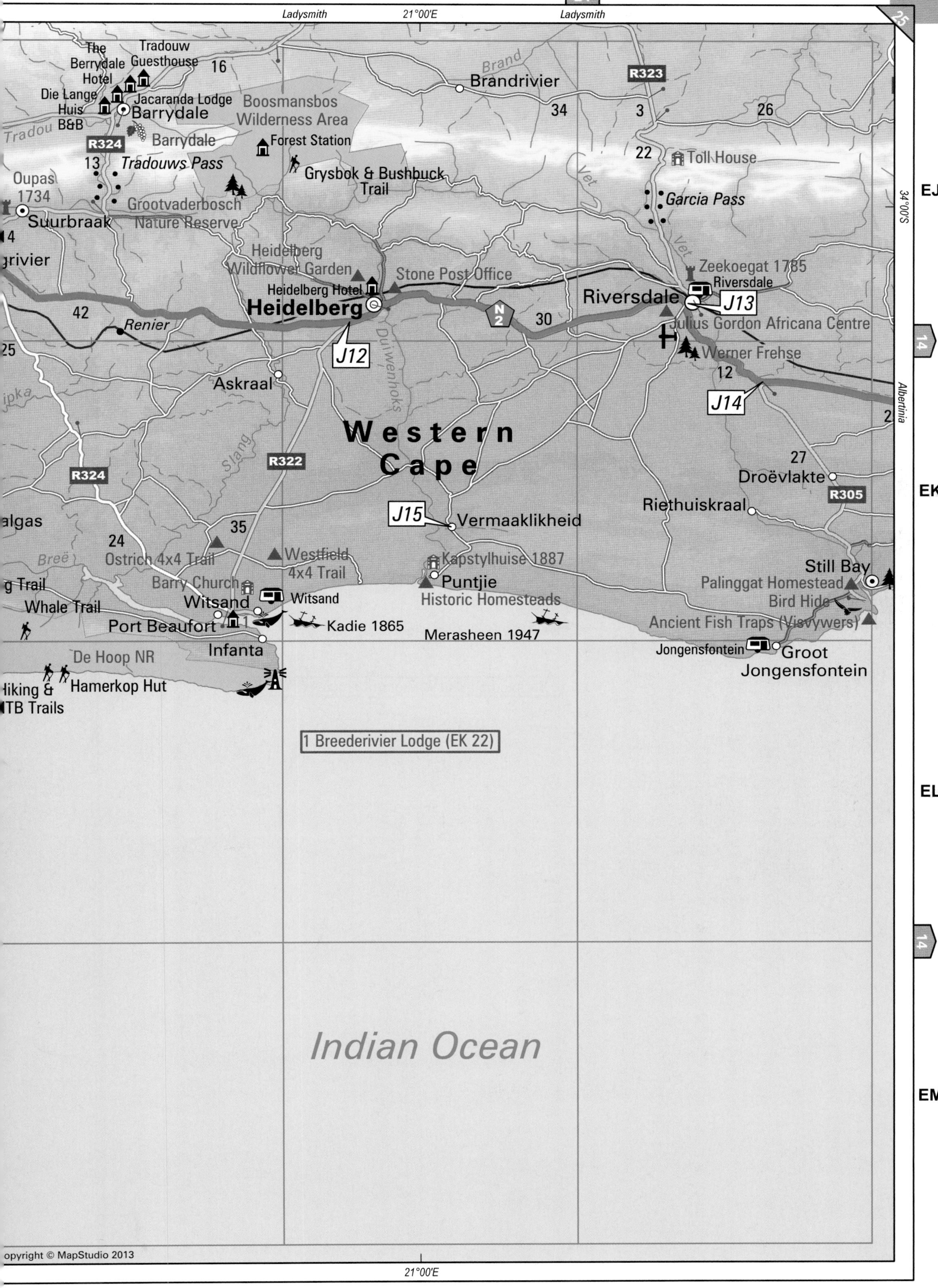

2.5 5   10   15   20 Kilometers

Ladysmith   21°00'E   Ladysmith

The Berrydale Hotel
Tradouw Guesthouse
Die Lange Huis B&B
Jacaranda Lodge
16
Barrydale
Boosmansbos Wilderness Area
R324
13
Barrydale
Tradouws Pass
Forest Station
Oupas 1734
Grysbok & Bushbuck Trail
Suurbraak
Grootvadersbosch Nature Reserve
grivier

Brand
Brandrivier
34
R323
3
26
22
Toll House
Garcia Pass

Heidelberg Wildflower Garden
Stone Post Office
Heidelberg Hotel
Heidelberg
Zeekoegat 1785
Riversdale
Riversdale
J13
J12
42
Renier
25
N2
30
Julius Gordon Africana Centre
Werner Frehse
12
J14

Askraal

W e s t e r n C a p e

Droëvlakte
R305

Riethuiskraal

J15
Vermaaklikheid

ipka
R324
35

algas
24
Ostrich 4x4 Trail
Breë
Westfield 4x4 Trail
Kapstylhuise 1887
Puntjie
Historic Homesteads
Still Bay
Palinggat Homestead
Bird Hide
Ancient Fish Traps (Visvywers)

g Trail
Whale Trail
Barry Church
Witsand
Witsand
Kadie 1865
Merasheen 1947
Jongensfontein
Groot Jongensfontein

Port Beaufort
1
Infanta

De Hoop NR

Hiking & TB Trails
Hamerkop Hut

1 Breederivier Lodge (EK 22)

Indian Ocean

EJ

34°00'S

14

EK

EL

14

EM

Albertinia
2

21°00'E

25   25   26   27

22°00'E *Oudtshoorn*

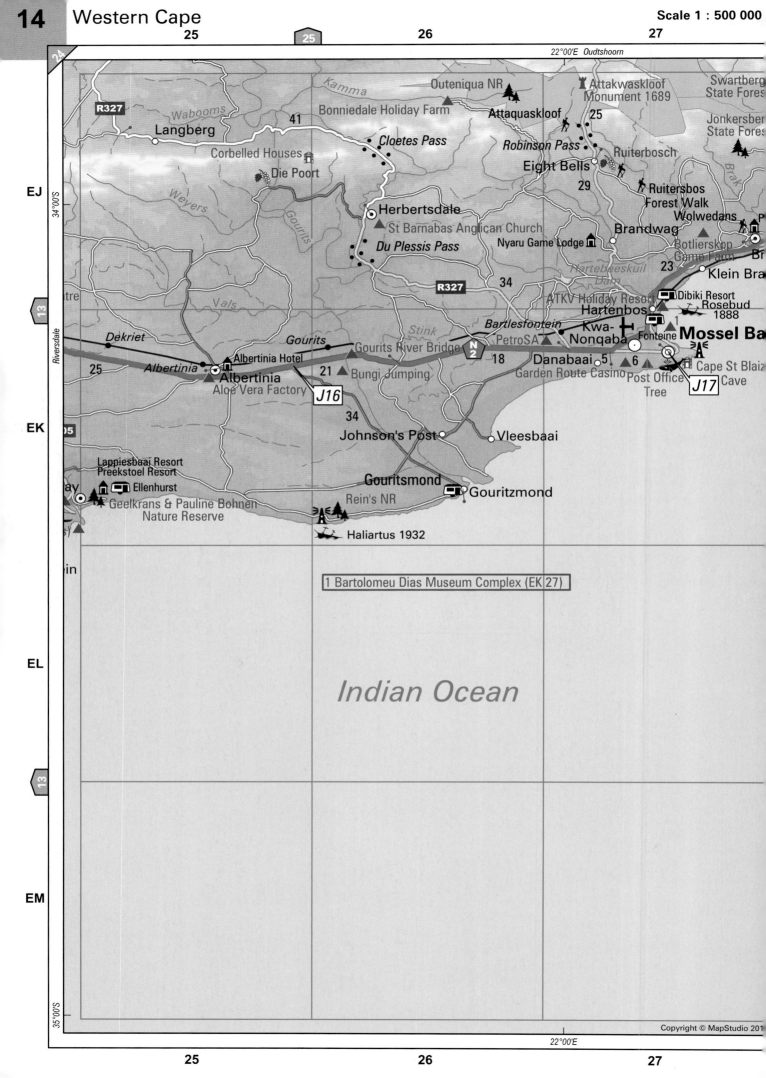

R327

Langberg

Corbelled Houses

Die Poort

Kamma

Outeniqua NR

Bonniedale Holiday Farm

Cloetes Pass

41

Waboombs

Weyers

Gourits

Attakwaskloof
Monument 1689

Attaquaskloof

25

Robinson Pass

Ruiterbosch

Eight Bells

29

Ruitersbos
Forest Walk

Wolwedans

Swartberg
State Fores

Jonkersber
State Fores

EJ

34°00'S

Herbertsdale

St Barnabas Anglican Church

Du Plessis Pass

Nyaru Game Lodge

Brandwag

Hartebeeskuil Dam

Botlierskop
Game Farm

23

Klein Bra

Br

Vals

Stink

R327

34

ATKV Holiday Resort

Hartenbos

Dibiki Resort
Rosebud
1888

13

Riversdale

Dekriet

Gourits

Gourits River Bridge

Bartlesfontein

PetroSA

Kwa-
Nonqaba

Fonteine

Mossel Ba

Albertinia Hotel

25

Albertinia

Albertinia

Aloe Vera Factory

J16

21

Bungi Jumping

N2

18

Danabaai

5

6

Garden Route Casino

Post Office
Tree

Cape St Blaiz
Cave

J17

EK

34

Johnson's Post

Vleesbaai

Lappiesbaai Resort
Preekstoel Resort

Ellenhurst

Geelkrans & Pauline Bohnen
Nature Reserve

ay

05

Gouritsmond

Rein's NR

Gouritzmond

Haliartus 1932

1 Bartolomeu Dias Museum Complex (EK 27)

EL

Indian Ocean

13

EM

35°00'S

25   26   27

22°00'E

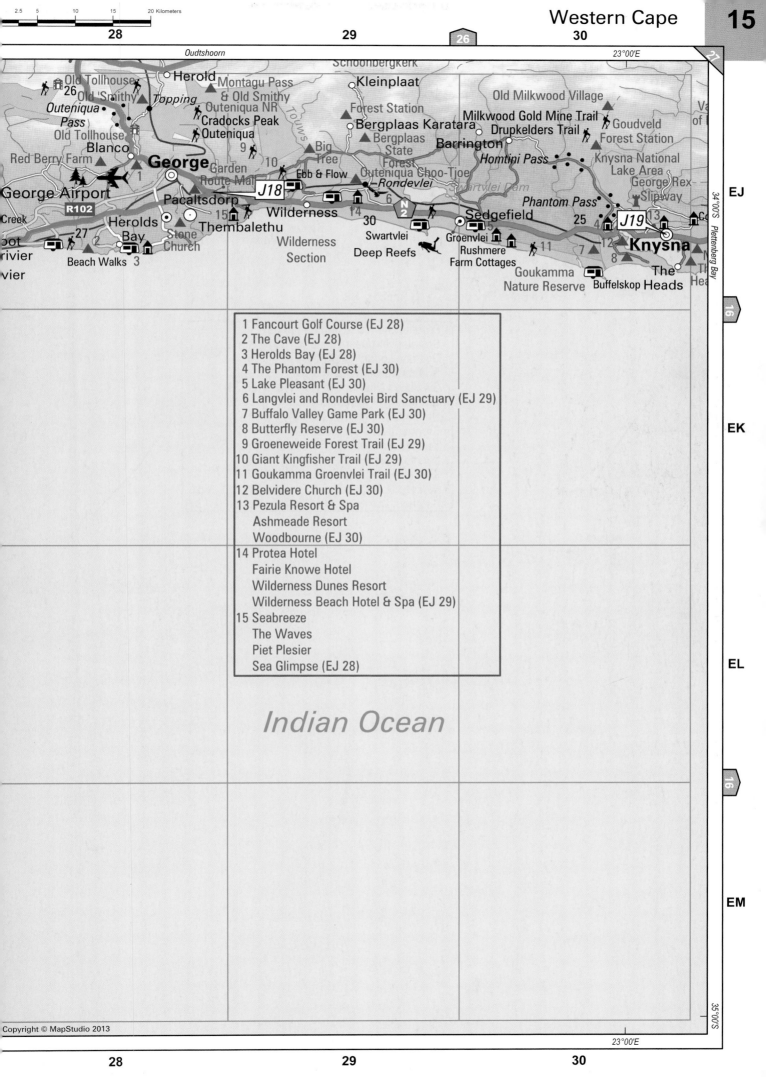

1 Fancourt Golf Course (EJ 28)
2 The Cave (EJ 28)
3 Herolds Bay (EJ 28)
4 The Phantom Forest (EJ 30)
5 Lake Pleasant (EJ 30)
6 Langvlei and Rondevlei Bird Sanctuary (EJ 29)
7 Buffalo Valley Game Park (EJ 30)
8 Butterfly Reserve (EJ 30)
9 Groeneweide Forest Trail (EJ 29)
10 Giant Kingfisher Trail (EJ 29)
11 Goukamma Groenvlei Trail (EJ 30)
12 Belvidere Church (EJ 30)
13 Pezula Resort & Spa
    Ashmeade Resort
    Woodbourne (EJ 30)
14 Protea Hotel
    Fairie Knowe Hotel
    Wilderness Dunes Resort
    Wilderness Beach Hotel & Spa (EJ 29)
15 Seabreeze
    The Waves
    Piet Plesier
    Sea Glimpse (EJ 28)

Indian Ocean

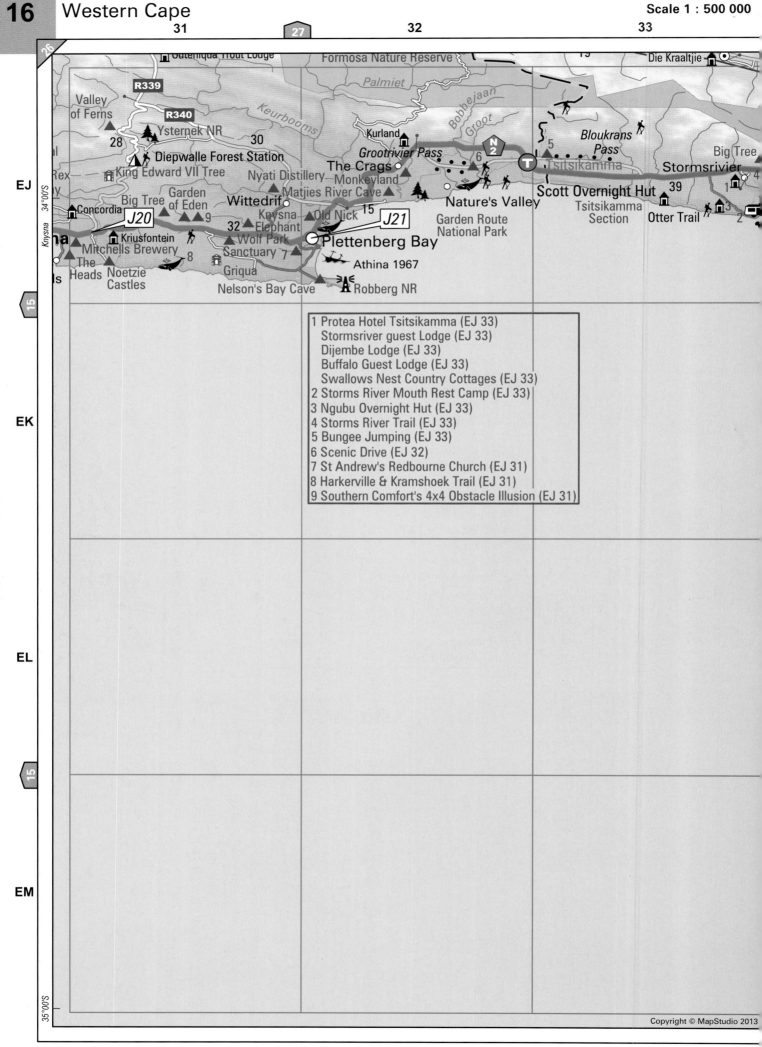

1 Protea Hotel Tsitsikamma (EJ 33)
  Stormsriver guest Lodge (EJ 33)
  Dijembe Lodge (EJ 33)
  Buffalo Guest Lodge (EJ 33)
  Swallows Nest Country Cottages (EJ 33)
2 Storms River Mouth Rest Camp (EJ 33)
3 Ngubu Overnight Hut (EJ 33)
4 Storms River Trail (EJ 33)
5 Bungee Jumping (EJ 33)
6 Scenic Drive (EJ 32)
7 St Andrew's Redbourne Church (EJ 31)
8 Harkerville & Kramshoek Trail (EJ 31)
9 Southern Comfort's 4x4 Obstacle Illusion (EJ 31)

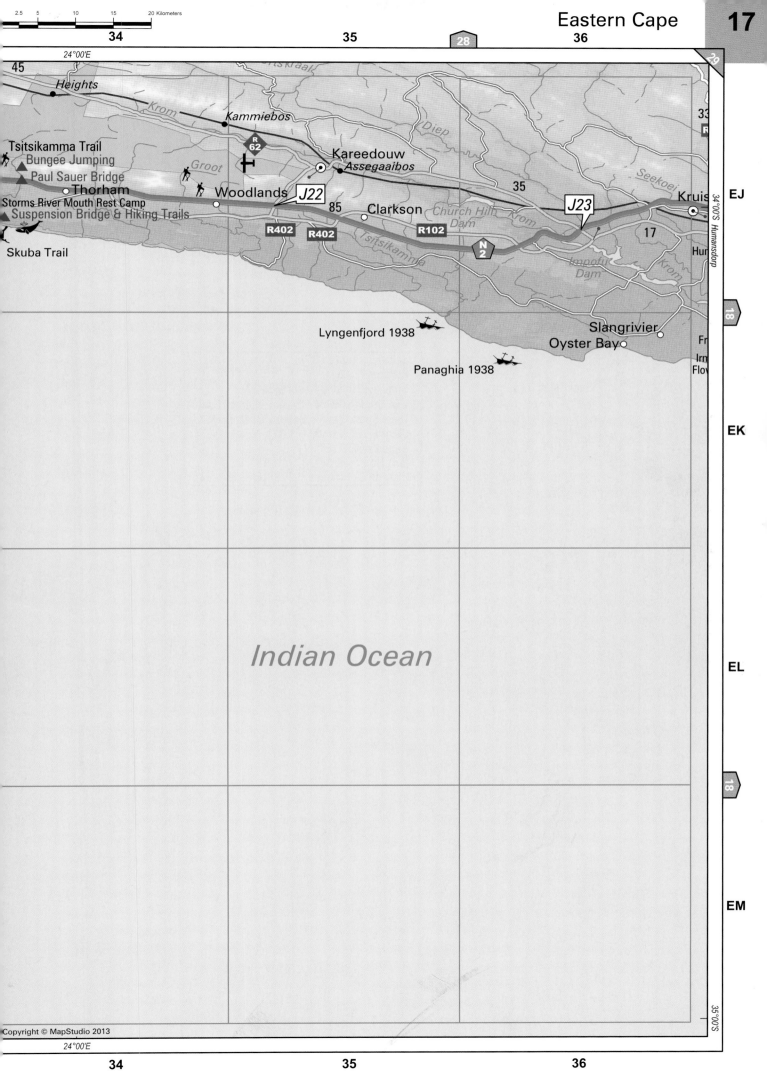

2.5 5 10 15 20 Kilometers

34   **35**   28   **36**   29

24°00'E

45
Heights
Krom
Kammiebos
R 62
Kareedouw
Assegaaibos
Tsitsikamma Trail
Bungee Jumping
Paul Sauer Bridge
Thorham
Woodlands J22 35
Storms River Mouth Rest Camp 85 Clarkson
Suspension Bridge & Hiking Trails
R402 R402
Skuba Trail *Tsitsikamma* R102
Church Hill Dam
N2
J23
Impofu Dam
17
33
EJ
34°00'S *Humansdorp*
Krom
Kruis
Hu

Lyngenfjord 1938
Slangrivier
Panaghia 1938 Oyster Bay
Fr
Irn
Flo
Groot
Diep
Seekoei

18

EK

Indian Ocean

EL

18

EM

Copyright © MapStudio 2013

24°00'E

35°00'S

34   **35**   **36**

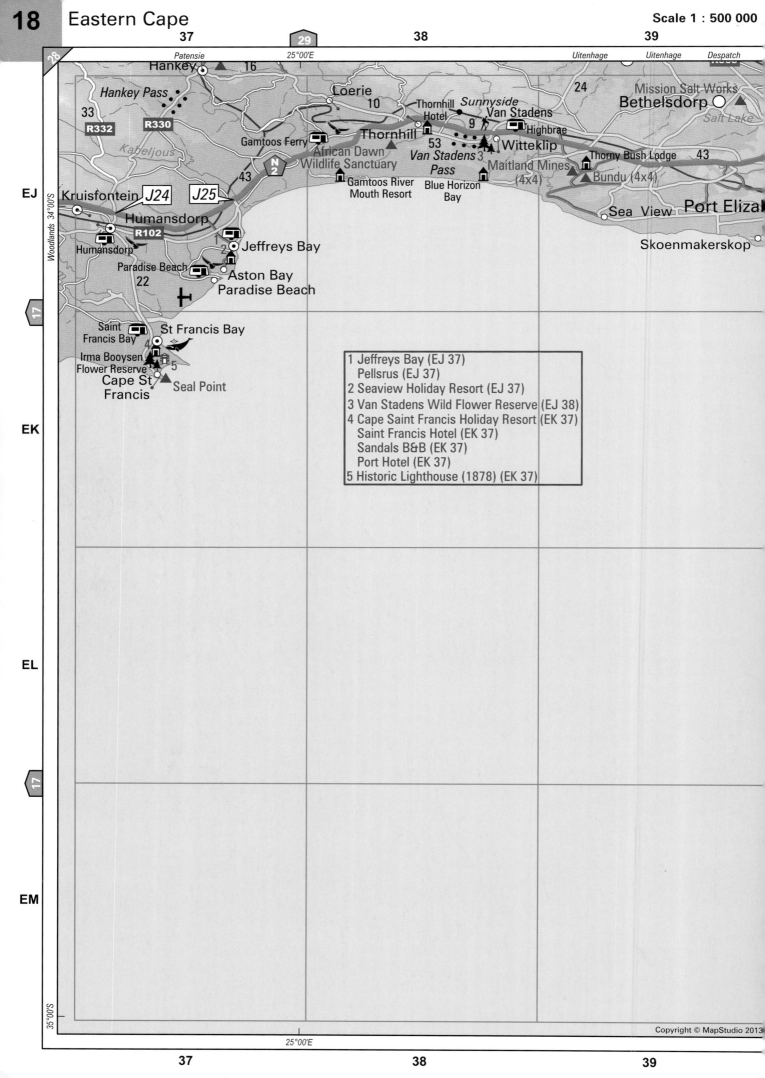

1 Jeffreys Bay (EJ 37)
  Pellsrus (EJ 37)
2 Seaview Holiday Resort (EJ 37)
3 Van Stadens Wild Flower Reserve (EJ 38)
4 Cape Saint Francis Holiday Resort (EK 37)
  Saint Francis Hotel (EK 37)
  Sandals B&B (EK 37)
  Port Hotel (EK 37)
5 Historic Lighthouse (1878) (EK 37)

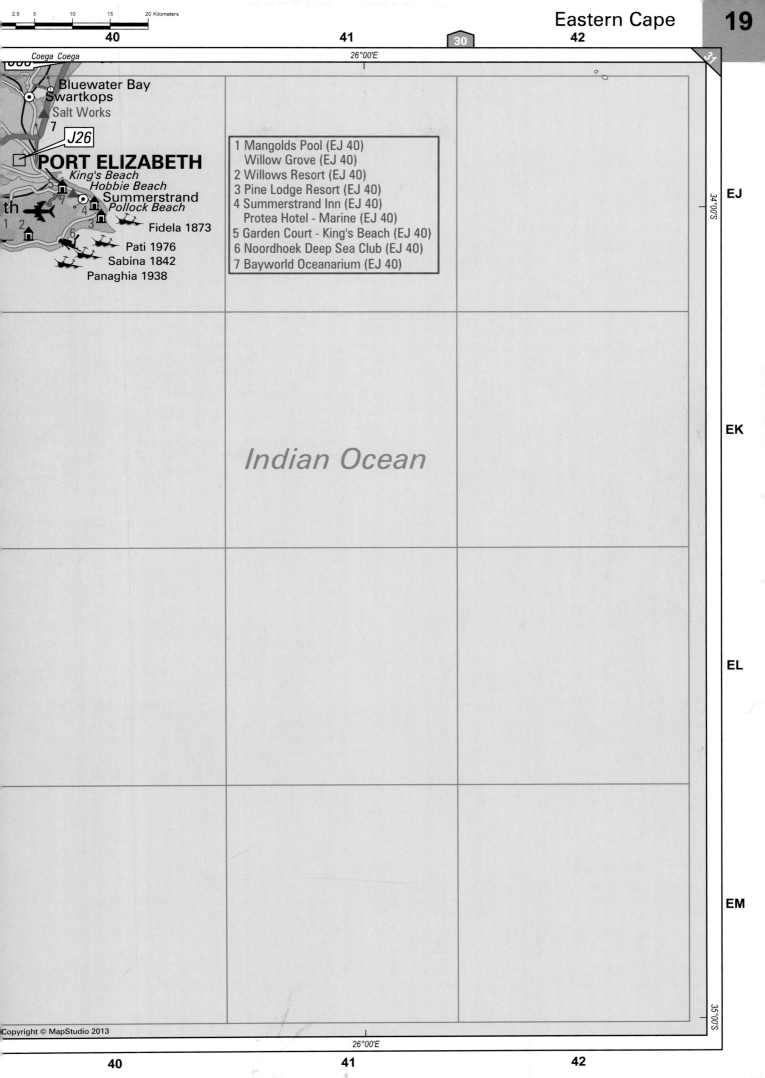

2.5 5   10   15   20 Kilometers
40   **41**   30   **42**

Coega Coega   26°00'E   31

Bluewater Bay
Swartkops
Salt Works

7

J26

PORT ELIZABETH
King's Beach
Hobbie Beach
Summerstrand
Pollock Beach

Fidela 1873

Pati 1976

Sabina 1842

Panaghia 1938

1 Mangolds Pool (EJ 40)
  Willow Grove (EJ 40)
2 Willows Resort (EJ 40)
3 Pine Lodge Resort (EJ 40)
4 Summerstrand Inn (EJ 40)
  Protea Hotel - Marine (EJ 40)
5 Garden Court - King's Beach (EJ 40)
6 Noordhoek Deep Sea Club (EJ 40)
7 Bayworld Oceanarium (EJ 40)

EJ

34°00'S

Indian Ocean

EK

EL

EM

35°00'S

26°00'E

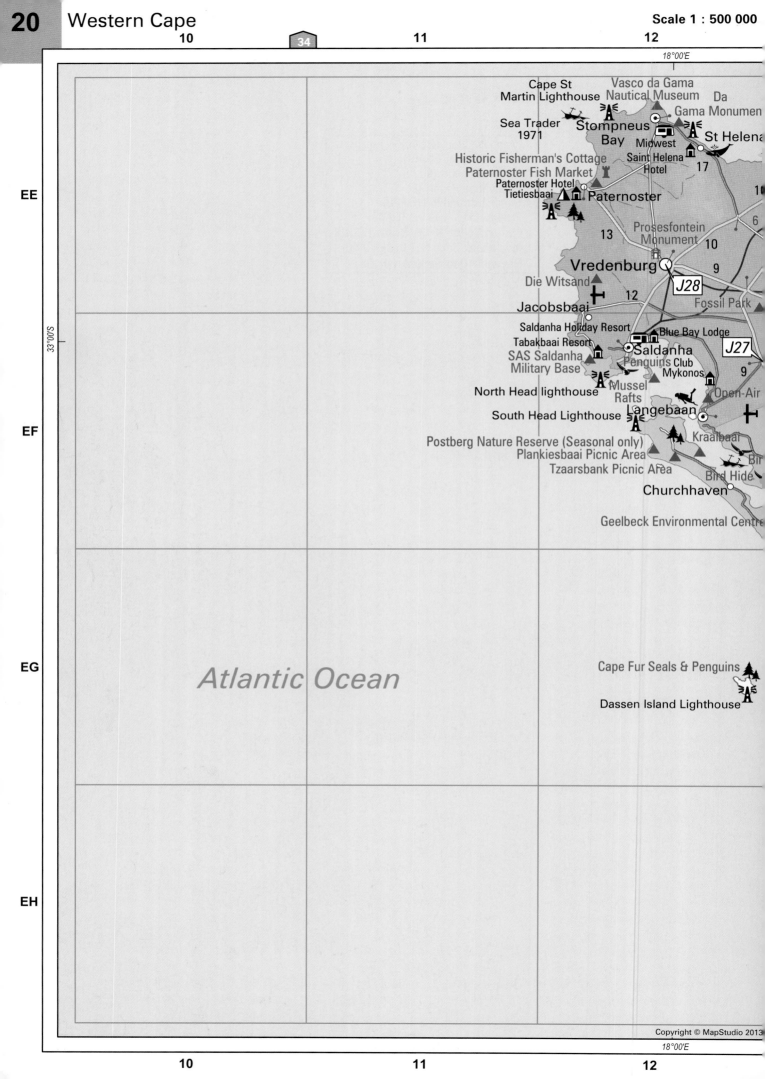

10   11   12

18°00'E

Cape St
Martin Lighthouse

Vasco da Gama
Nautical Museum

Da
Gama Monumen

Sea Trader
1971

Stompneus
Bay

Midwest

St Helena

Saint Helena
Hotel

17

EE

Historic Fisherman's Cottage
Paternoster Fish Market

Paternoster Hotel

Tietiesbaai

Paternoster

Prosesfontein
Monument

13

10

Vredenburg

9

Die Witsand

J28

12

Jacobsbaai

Fossil Park

33°00'S

Saldanha Holiday Resort

Tabakbaai Resort

Blue Bay Lodge

J27

SAS Saldanha

Saldanha

Military Base

Penguins Club

9

Mykonos

EF

North Head lighthouse

Mussel
Rafts

Open-Air

South Head Lighthouse

Langebaan

Postberg Nature Reserve (Seasonal only)

Kraalbaai

Plankiesbaai Picnic Area

Bir

Tzaarsbank Picnic Area

Bird Hide

Churchhaven

Geelbeck Environmental Centre

EG

Atlantic Ocean

Cape Fur Seals & Penguins

Dassen Island Lighthouse

EH

18°00'E

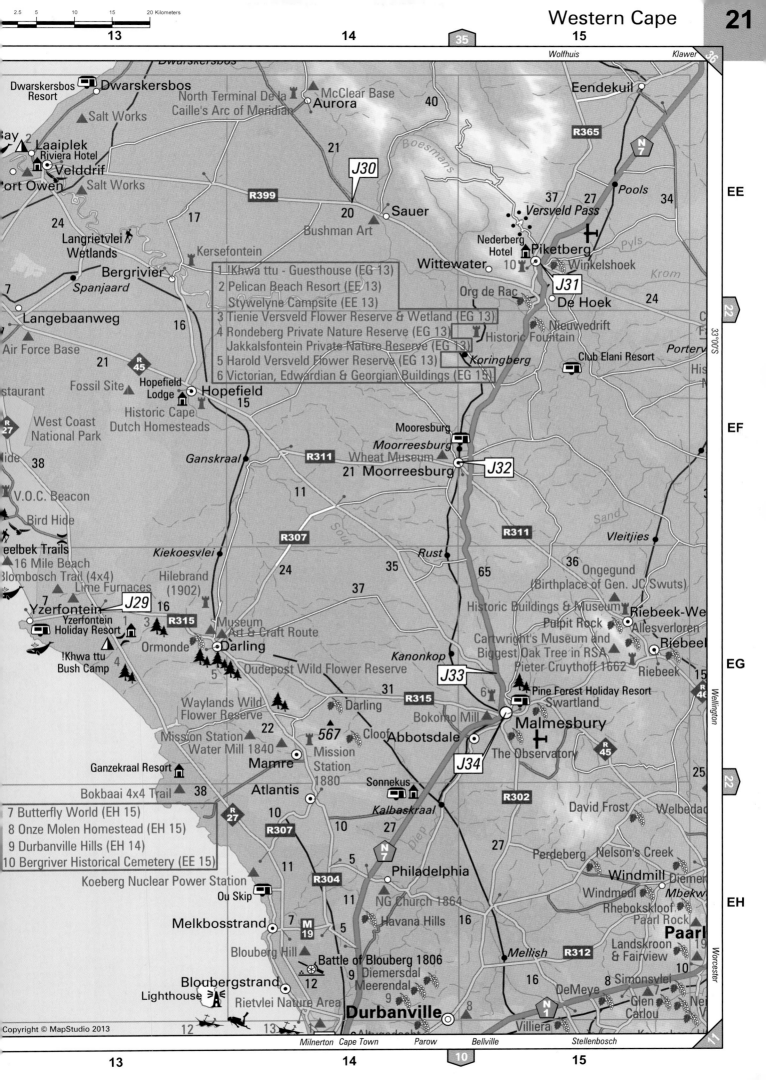

2.5 5   10   15   20 Kilometers

13   **14**   35   **15**

Wolfhuis   Klawer

Dwarskersbos
Dwarskersbos ▲ Dwarskersbos   North Terminal De la   McClear Base   Eendekuil
Resort   Caille's Arc of Meridian   Aurora   40   R365
▲ Salt Works
ay 2   N7
△ Laaiplek   37   27   Pools   34
  Riviera Hotel   21   Versveld Pass
Velddrif   J30
ort Owen ▲ Salt Works   20   Sauer   Nederberg   Piketberg
24   17   Bushman Art   Hotel   10   Wittewater   Winkelshoek   J31
Langrietvlei   R399   De Hoek   24
Wetlands   Kersefontein   Org de Rac   Nieuwedrift
Bergrivier   Historic Fountain   Porterv
7   Spanjaard   1 !Khwa ttu - Guesthouse (EG 13)   Koringberg   Club Elani Resort   His
Langebaanweg   16   2 Pelican Beach Resort (EE 13)
Air Force Base   R   Stywelyne Campsite (EE 13)
staurant   45   21   3 Tienie Versveld Flower Reserve & Wetland (EG 13)
R   Fossil Site   Hopefield   4 Rondeberg Private Nature Reserve (EG 13)
27   Lodge   Hopefield   Jakkalsfontein Private Nature Reserve (EG 13)
West Coast   15   5 Harold Versveld Flower Reserve (EG 13)   EF
National Park   Historic Cape   6 Victorian, Edwardian & Georgian Buildings (EG 15)
ide   38   Dutch Homesteads   Mooresburg
Ganskraal   R311   Moorreesburg   J32
V.O.C. Beacon   Wheat Museum
Bird Hide   11   21 Moorreesburg   R311   Vleitjies
eelbek Trails   R307   Rust   36
▲ 16 Mile Beach   Kiekoesvlei   24   35   65   Ongegund
lombosch Trail (4x4)   (Birthplace of Gen. JC Swuts)
Lime Furnaces   Hilebrand   37   Historic Buildings & Museum
7   Yzerfontein   J29   16   (1902)   Pulpit Rock   Riebeek-We   EG
△ Yzerfontein   Museum   Cartwright's Museum and   Allesverloren
Holiday Resort   3   R315   Art & Craft Route   Kanonkop   Biggest Oak Tree in RSA   Riebeel
!Khwa ttu   Ormonde   Darling   J33   Pieter Cruythoff 1662   Riebeek
Bush Camp   4   5   Oudepost Wild Flower Reserve   6   Pine Forest Holiday Resort
31   Darling   R315   Swartland   EG
Waylands Wild   Bokomo Mill   Malmesbury
Flower Reserve   567   Cloof   Abbotsdale   The Observatory   R   25
Ganzekraal Resort   22   Mission   Sonnekus   J34   45
Mission Station   Station   David Frost
Water Mill 1840   Mamre   1880   R302
Bokbaai 4x4 Trail   38   Atlantis   Kalbaskraal   27   Perdeberg   Nelson's Creek
7 Butterfly World (EH 15)   10   27   Windmill Diemer
8 Onze Molen Homestead (EH 15)   R   10   Windmoul   Mbekw
9 Durbanville Hills (EH 14)   27   5   Philadelphia   Rhebokskloof
10 Bergriver Historical Cemetery (EE 15)   11   NG Church 1864   16   Paarl Rock
Koeberg Nuclear Power Station   R304   11   Havana Hills   16   Paarl   EH
Ou Skip   M   5   Landskroon
Melkbosstrand   7   19   DeMeye   & Fairview   19
Blouberg Hill   Mellish   R312
Bloubergstrand   Battle of Blouberg 1806   16   8 Simonsvlei   10
Lighthouse   12   Diemersdal   Villiera   Glen
Rietvlei Nature Area   9   Meerendal   N   Carlou
Durbanville   Altugedacht   1

Copyright © MapStudio 2013   12   13

Milnerton Cape Town   Parow   Bellville   Stellenbosch

13   **14**   10   **15**

EE

22

EF

EG

22

EH

Worcester

33°00'S

36

16 36 17 18

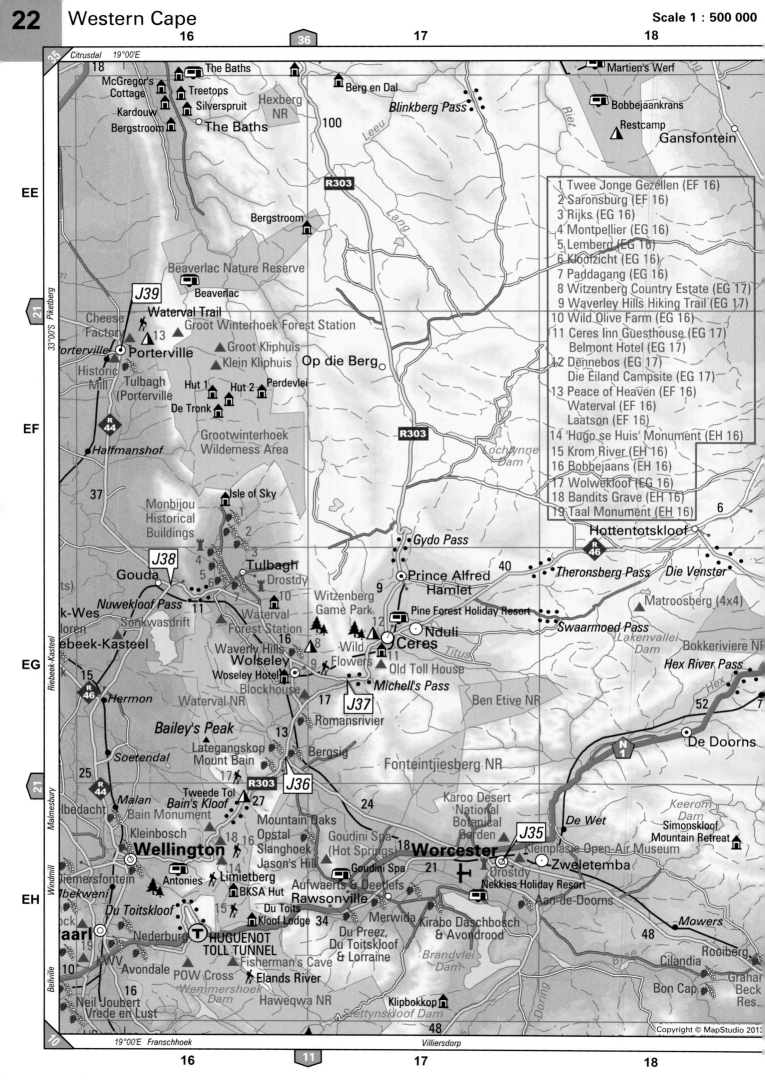

35 Citrusdal 19°00'E
18

McGregor's Cottage
The Baths
Treetops
Kardouw
Silverspruit
Bergstroom
Hexberg NR
The Baths
Berg en Dal
Blinkberg Pass
Martien's Werf
Bobbejaankrans
Restcamp
Gansfontein

EE

R303
100

21 Piketberg
33°00'S

Bergstroom

Beaverlac Nature Reserve
Beaverlac

J39
Waterval Trail
Cheese Factory
Porterville 13
Porterville
Groot Winterhoek Forest Station
Groot Kliphuis
Klein Kliphuis
Op die Berg

EF

Historic Mill
Tulbagh (Porterville
Halfmanshof
R44
Hut 1 Hut 2 Perdevlei
De Tronk

Grootwinterhoek Wilderness Area

37

Monbijou Historical Buildings
Isle of Sky
1
2

J38
Gouda
4
5
6
11
Nuwekloof Pass
Sonkwasdrift
7
Tulbagh
Drostdy
10
Waterval Forest Station
Witzenberg Game Park
16
8
Waverly Hills
9
Wild Flowers
Wolseley
Woseley Hotel
11
Blockhouse
Waterval NR
17

Lochlynne Dam

Gydo Pass
Prince Alfred Hamlet
9
Pine Forest Holiday Resort
12
Nduli
Ceres
Old Toll House

Hottentotskloof
R46
40
Theronsberg Pass
Die Venster
Matroosberg (4x4)
Swaarmoed Pass
Lakenvallei Dam
Bokkeriviere NR
Hex River Pass

EG

Riebeek-Kasteel
k-Wes
loren
iebeek-Kasteel
15
R46
Hermon

Bailey's Peak
Lategangskop
Mount Bain
Soetendal
13
Bergsig
Romansrivier
J37
Michell's Pass
Ben Etive NR
Fonteintjiesberg NR
52 7
De Doorns
N1

21 Malmesbury

25
R44
Malan
ilbedacht
Bain Monument
Kleinbosch
Tweede Tol
Bain's Kloof
27
Mountain Oaks
Opstal
Slanghoek
17
R303
J36
24
Karoo Desert National Botanical Garden
De Wet
Keerom Dam
Simonskloof Mountain Retreat
J35
Kleinplasie Open-Air Museum
Zweletemba
Worcester
21

EH

Windmill
Wellington
18 16
Antonies 14
Limietberg
BKSA Hut
Jason's Hill
Goudini Spa (Hot Springs)
Goudini Spa
18
Drostdy
Nekkies Holiday Resort
Aan-de-Doorns
Mowers
48
Rooiberg

Diemersfontein
Ibekweni
Du Toitskloof
15
Du Toits
Kloof Lodge 34
Aufwaerts & Deetlefs
Rawsonville
Merwida
Kirabo Daschbosch & Avondrood
Du Preez, Du Toitskloof & Lorraine
Brandvlei Dam
Cilandia
Bon Cap
Grahar Beck Res.

aarl
Nederburg
HUGUENOT TOLL TUNNEL
T
Fisherman's Cave
Elands River
Klipbokkop

10 ck
19
Avondale
POW Cross
Neil Joubert
Vrede en Lust
16
Wemmershoek Dam
Haweqwa NR
Klipbokkop
Stettynskloof Dam

10 Bellville
19°00'E Franschhoek
Villiersdorp
48

16 11 17 18

Index listing (right panel):

1 Twee Jonge Gezellen (EF 16)
2 Saronsburg (EF 16)
3 Rijks (EG 16)
4 Montpellier (EG 16)
5 Lemberg (EG 16)
6 Kloofzicht (EG 16)
7 Paddagang (EG 16)
8 Witzenberg Country Estate (EG 17)
9 Waverley Hills Hiking Trail (EG 17)
10 Wild Olive Farm (EG 16)
11 Ceres Inn Guesthouse (EG 17)
   Belmont Hotel (EG 17)
12 Dennebos (EG 17)
   Die Eiland Campsite (EG 17)
13 Peace of Heaven (EF 16)
   Waterval (EF 16)
   Laatson (EF 16)
14 'Hugo se Huis' Monument (EH 16)
15 Krom River (EH 16)
16 Bobbejaans (EH 16)
17 Wolwekloof (EG 16)
18 Bandits Grave (EH 16)
19 Taal Monument (EH 16)

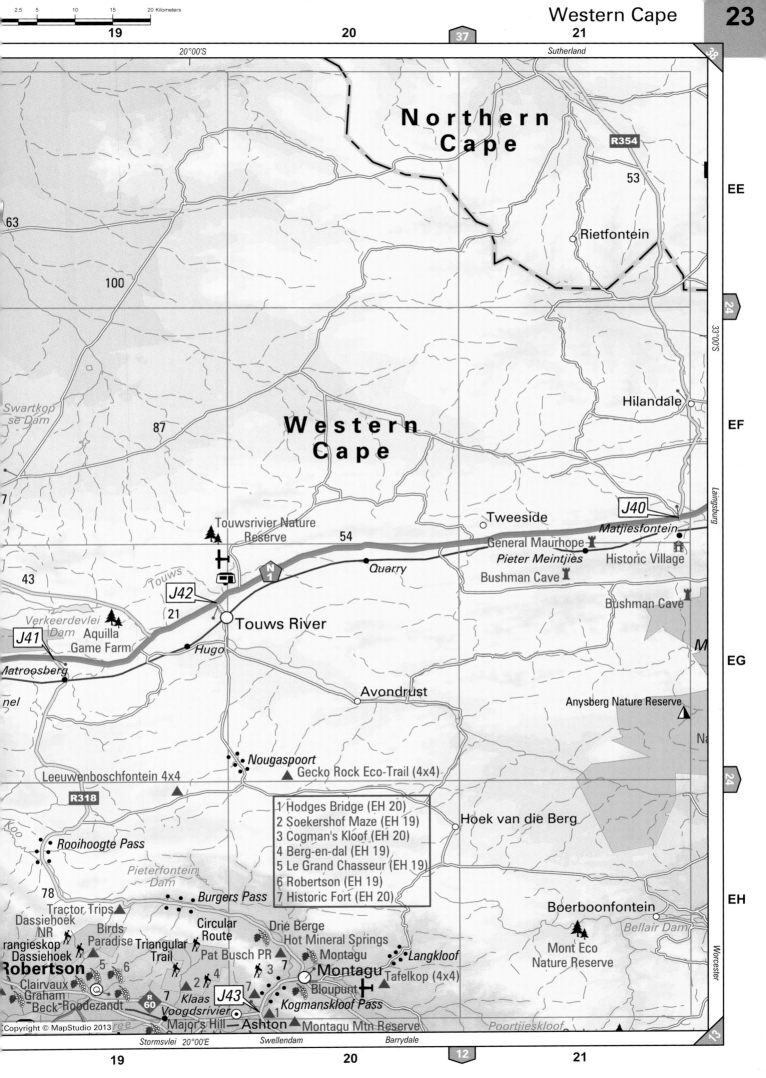

2.5 5 10 15 20 Kilometers

19   **20**   37   **21**

20°00'S   Sutherland

N o r t h e r n
C a p e

R354

EE

53

Rietfontein

63

24   33°00'S

100

Hilandale   EF

Swartkop
se Dam

W e s t e r n
C a p e

87

7

Touwsrivier Nature
Reserve

Tweeside   J40   Matjiesfontein

General Maurhope   Laingsburg

54   Pieter Meintjies   Historic Village

43   Quarry   Bushman Cave

N1   Bushman Cave

J42   EG

21

Verkeerdevlei
Dam   Aquilla
Game Farm

J41

Touws River

Hugo

Matroosberg   M

nel   Avondrust   Anysberg Nature Reserve

24

Na

Nougaspoort   Hoek van die Berg

Leeuwenboschfontein 4x4   Gecko Rock Eco-Trail (4x4)

R318

Koo   1 Hodges Bridge (EH 20)
2 Soekershof Maze (EH 19)
Rooihoogte Pass   3 Cogman's Kloof (EH 20)
4 Berg-en-dal (EH 19)
5 Le Grand Chasseur (EH 19)
6 Robertson (EH 19)
7 Historic Fort (EH 20)

Pieterfontein
Dam

78   Boerboonfontein   EH

Burgers Pass   Bellair Dam

Tractor Trips
Dassiehoek   Circular   Drie Berge   Mont Eco
NR   Route   Hot Mineral Springs   Nature Reserve
rangieskop   Birds   Triangular   Montagu
Dassiehoek   Paradise   Trail   Pat Busch PR   Langkloof
Robertson   3 7   Montagu   Tafelkop (4x4)
5   2 4   7   Worcester
Clairvaux   1   Bloupunt
Graham   7   Klaas
Beck Roodezandt   R60   Voogdsrivier   J43   Kogmanskloof Pass
Major's Hill   Ashton   Montagu Mtn Reserve   Poortjieskloof
ree   Stormsvlei 20°00'E   Swellendam   Barrydale   13

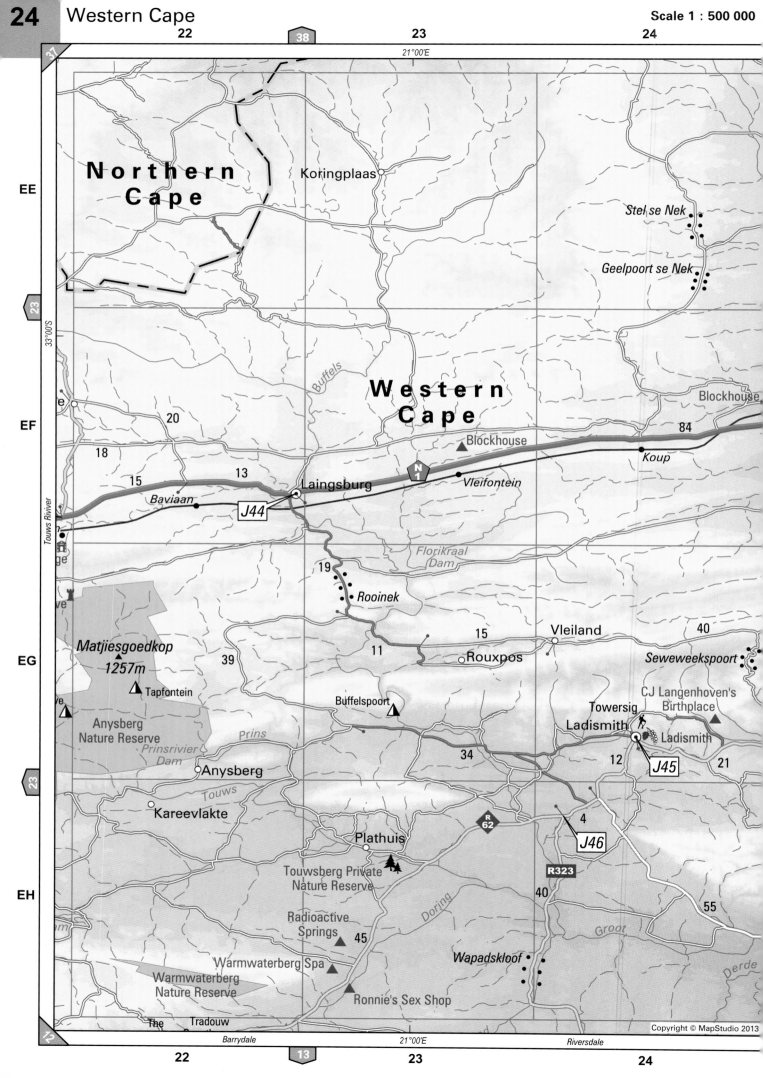

Northern Cape

Koringplaas

Stel se Nek

Geelpoort se Nek

Western Cape

Blockhouse

Buffels

20

Blockhouse

18

84

Blockhouse

15

13

Koup

Baviaan

Laingsburg

Vleifontein

J44

Florikraal Dam

19

Rooinek

15

Vleiland

40

11

Rouxpos

Seweeweekspoort

Matjiesgoedkop
1257m

39

Tapfontein

Buffelspoort

CJ Langenhoven's Birthplace

Towersig
Ladismith

Anysberg
Nature Reserve

Prins

34

Ladismith

Prinsrivier Dam

12

J45

21

Anysberg

Touws

Kareevlakte

4

J46

Plathuis

R62

Touwsberg Private Nature Reserve

Doring

R323

40

55

Radioactive Springs

45

Wapadskloof

Groot

Warmwaterberg Spa

Warmwaterberg Nature Reserve

Ronnie's Sex Shop

The

Tradouw

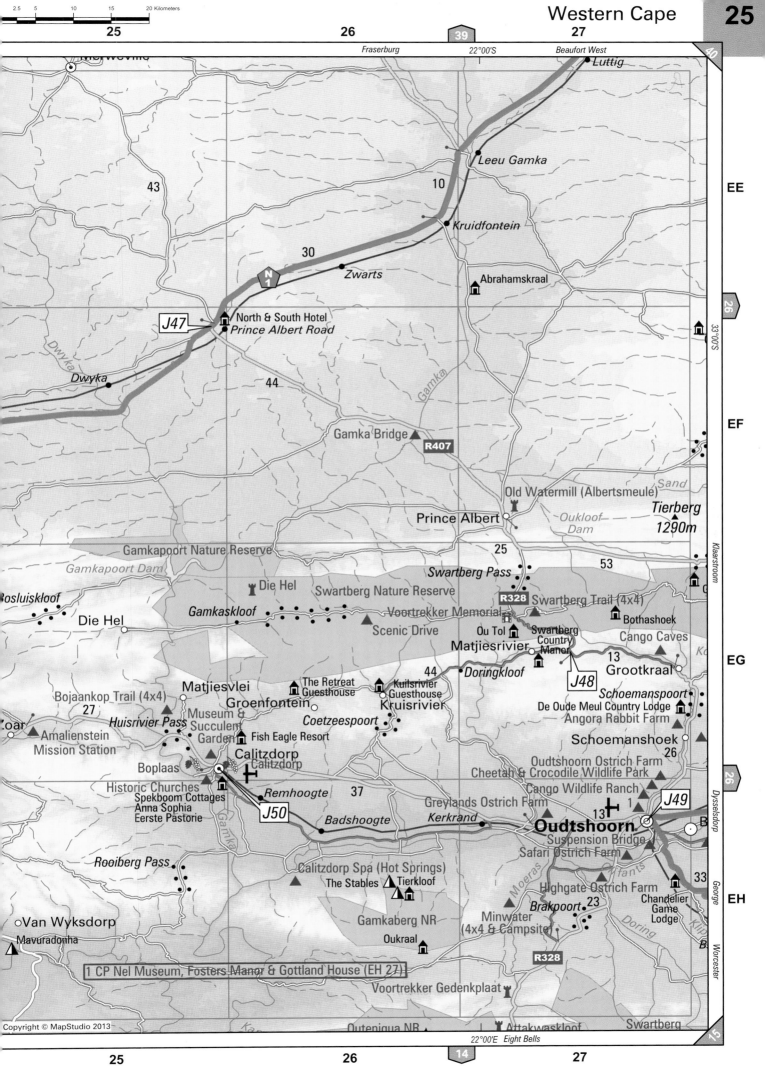

2.5 5   10   15   20 Kilometers

25   **26**   39   **27**

Fraserburg   22°00'S   Beaufort West

Luttig

EE

43

Leeu Gamka

10

Kruidfontein

30

Zwarts   Abrahamskraal

26

33°00'S

N 1

J47   North & South Hotel
Prince Albert Road

44

Dwyka

Dwyka   **EF**

Gamka

Gamka Bridge   R407

Sand

Old Watermill (Albertsmeule)

Prince Albert   *Oukloof Dam*   *Tierberg*
                                        1290m

25

Gamkapoort Nature Reserve   53

Gamkapoort Dam   *Swartberg Pass*

osluiskloof   Die Hel   Swartberg Nature Reserve   R328   Swartberg Trail (4x4)

Die Hel   *Gamkaskloof*   Voortrekker Memorial   Bothashoek   **EG**

Scenic Drive   Ou Tol   Swartberg
                                        Country Manor   Cango Caves

Matjiesrivier   J48   *Schoemanspoort*

44   *Doringkloof*   13   Grootkraal

Bojaankop Trail (4x4)   The Retreat   Kuilsrivier   De Oude Meul Country Lodge
                        Guesthouse   Guesthouse   Angora Rabbit Farm

27   Matjiesvlei   Groenfontein   Kruisrivier

Huisrivier Pass   Museum &   *Coetzeespoort*   Schoemanshoek
                        Succulent
oar   Amalienstein   Garden   Fish Eagle Resort   26
        Mission Station   Oudtshoorn Ostrich Farm
                                                Cheetah & Crocodile Wildlife Park
        Boplaas   Calitzdorp   Cango Wildlife Ranch
                        Calitzdorp
        Historic Churches   *Remhoogte*   37   Greylands Ostrich Farm   J49
        Spekboom Cottages
        Anna Sophia   J50   *Badshoogte*   *Kerkrand*   13   1   **Oudtshoorn**
        Eerste Pastorie   Suspension Bridge   B

Rooiberg Pass   Safari Ostrich Farm   33

                Calitzdorp Spa (Hot Springs)   Highgate Ostrich Farm   **EH**
                The Stables   Tierkloof   Chandelier
oVan Wyksdorp   Game
                Gamkaberg NR   Minwater   *Brakpoort*   23   Lodge
Mavuradonha   (4x4 & Campsite)
                        Oukraal

1 CP Nel Museum, Fosters Manor & Gottland House (EH 27)

Voortrekker Gedenkplaat

Qutenigua NR   *Attakwaskloof*   Swartberg

Copyright © MapStudio 2013   22°00'E   *Eight Bells*

25   **26**   14   **27**

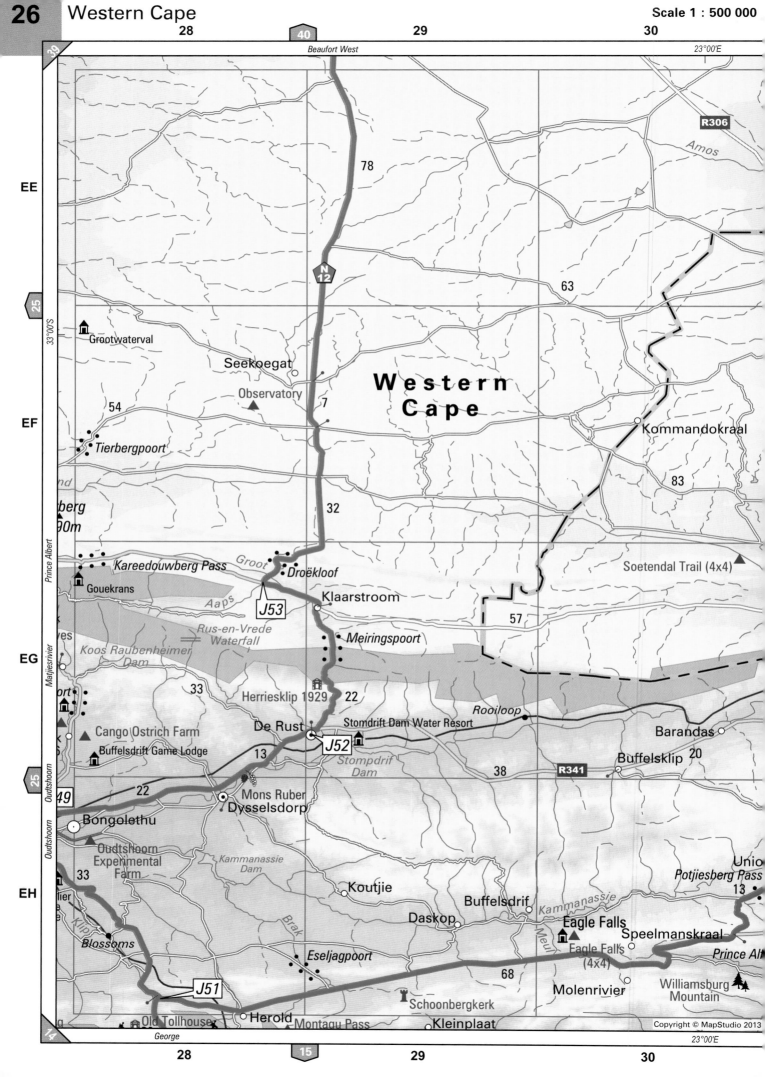

Western Cape

Beaufort West

R306

Amos

78

63

Grootwaterval

Seekoegat

Observatory

7

54

Kommandokraal

Tierbergpoort

83

32

Kareedouwberg Pass

Groot

Droëkloof

Soetendal Trail (4x4)

Gouekrans

Aaps

Klaarstroom

J53

Rus-en-Vrede
Waterfall

Meiringspoort

57

Koos Raubenheimer
Dam

33

Rooiloop

Herriesklip 1929

22

Barandas

De Rust

Stomdrift Dam Water Resort

Cango Ostrich Farm

J52

Buffelsklip 20

Buffelsdrift Game Lodge

13

Stompdrif
Dam

38

R341

22

Mons Ruber

Dysselsdorp

Bongolethu

49

Oudtshoorn
Experimental
Farm

Kammanassie
Dam

Unio

Potjiesberg Pass

33

Koutjie

13

Buffelsdrif

Kammanassie

Blossoms

Daskop

Eagle Falls

Speelmanskraal

Eseljagpoort

Eagle Falls
(4x4)

Prince Alb

68

Williamsburg
Mountain

J51

Molenrivier

Schoonbergkerk

Old Tollhouse

Herold

Montagu Pass

Kleinplaat

George

Copyright © MapStudio 2013

EE

25

33°00'S

EF

Prince Albert

EG

Matjiesrivier

25

Oudtshoorn

EH

39

40

28

29

30

23°00'E

15

23°00'E

14

N12

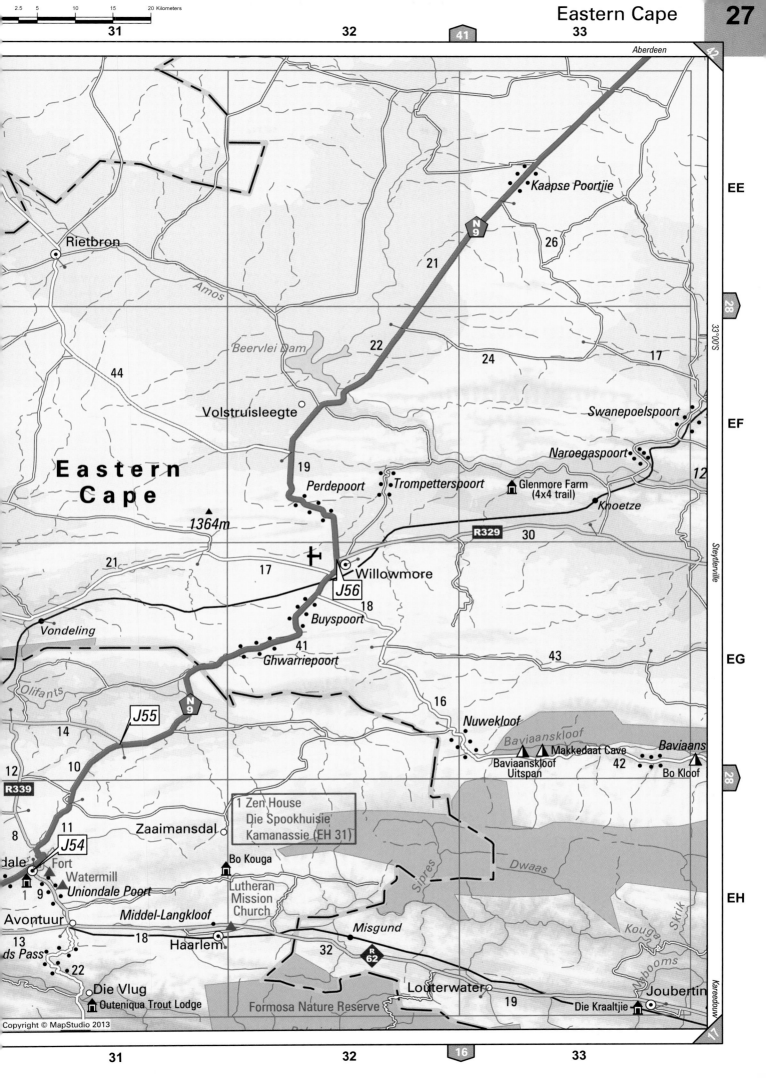

Aberdeen

2.5 5   10   15   20 Kilometers

31

32

41

33

42

28

33°00'S

EE

EF

EG

EH

28

17

Steytlerville

Kareedouw

Kaapse Poortjie

N9

26

21

22

24

17

Rietbron

Amos

Beervlei Dam

44

Swanepoelspoort

Naroegaspoort

Volstruisleegte

19

Perdepoort

Trompetterspoort

Glenmore Farm
(4x4 trail)

Knoetze

**E a s t e r n
C a p e**

▲
1364m

21

17

✝

Willowmore

J56

R329

30

18

Buyspoort

41

Ghwarriepoort

43

Vondeling

16

Nuwekloof

Baviaanskloof

Makkedaat Cave

Baviaans

Olifants

14

J55

N9

10

Baviaanskloof
Uitspan

42

Bo Kloof

12

R339

11

8

J54

dale

Fort

Watermill

Uniondale Poort

1   9

Zaaimansdal

1 Zen House
'Die Spookhuisie'
Kamanassie (EH 31)

Bo Kouga

Lutheran
Mission
Church

Sipres

Dwaas

Kouga

Skrik

Nabooms

Avontuur

13

ds Pass

22

Middel-Langkloof

18

Haarlem

Misgund

32

R62

19

Louterwater

Joubertin

Die Vlug

Outeniqua Trout Lodge

Formosa Nature Reserve

Die Kraaltjie

16

17

31

32

33

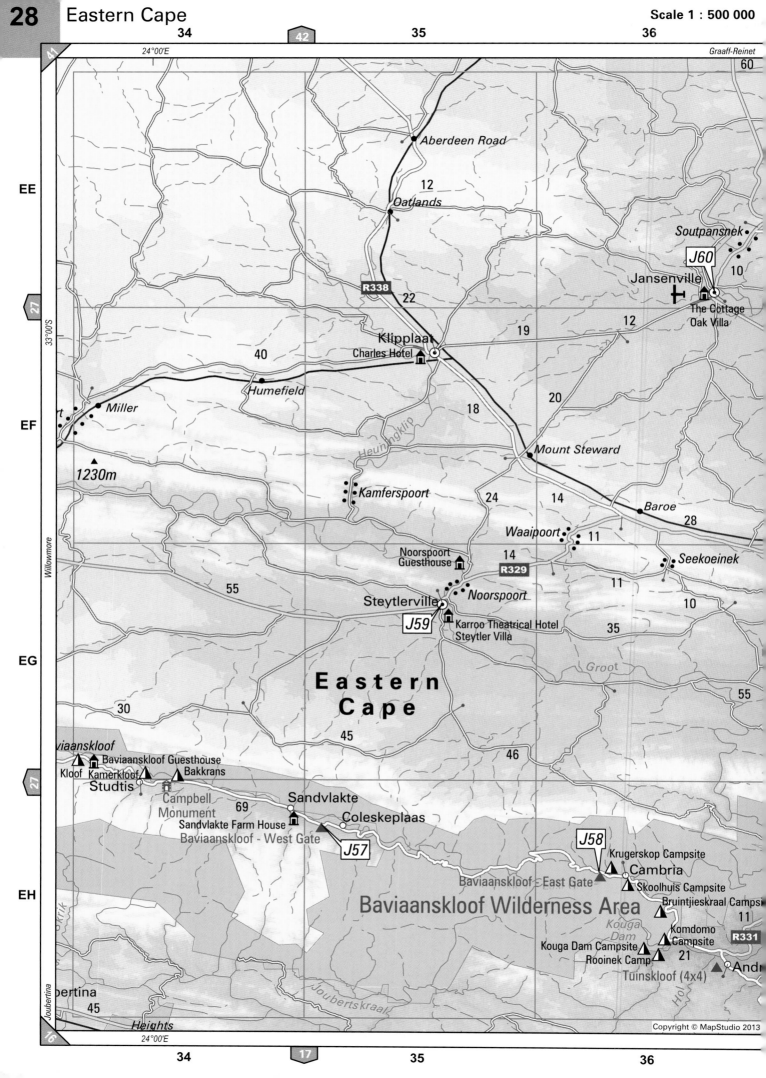

34 42 35 36

24°00'E Graaff-Reinet

41

60

EE

Aberdeen Road

12

Oatlands

Soutpansnek

J60

10

27

33°00'S

Jansenville

R338

22

The Cottage
Oak Villa

12

19

Klipplaat

EF

Miller

40

Charles Hotel

Humefield

18

20

Willowmore

1230m

Heuningklip

Mount Steward

Kamferspoort

24

14

Baroe

28

14

Waaipoort

11

Noorspoort
Guesthouse

14

Seekoeinek

R329

55

Noorspoort

11

Steytlerville

J59

11

10

EG

Karroo Theatrical Hotel
Steytler Villa

35

Groot

E a s t e r n
C a p e

30

45

55

46

27

viaanskloof

Baviaanskloof Guesthouse

Kloof Kamerkloof Bakkrans

Studtis

Campbell
Monument

Sandvlakte

69

Coleskeplaas

Sandvlakte Farm House

J57

Baviaanskloof - West Gate

J58

Krugerskop Campsite

Baviaanskloof - East Gate

Cambria

EH

Skoolhuis Campsite

Bruintjieskraal Campsi

Baviaanskloof Wilderness Area

11

Kouga
Dam

R331

Komdomo
Campsite

Kouga Dam Campsite

21

Rooinek Camp

And

Tuinskloof (4x4)

Joubertina

bertina

Joubertskraal

Hol

45

Heights

24°00'E

16 17

34 35 36

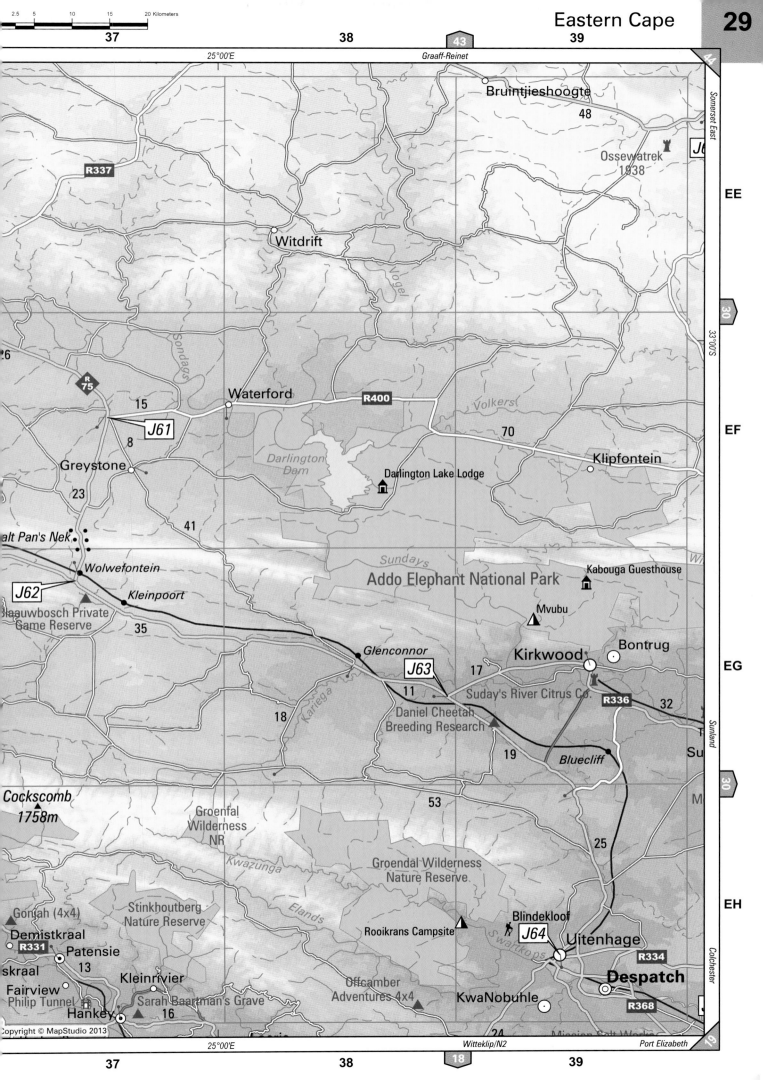

2.5 5   10   15   20 Kilometers

37   38   43   39
                                        Graaff-Reinet

25°00'E

Bruintjieshoogte

48

Ossewatrek
1938

EE

33°00'S

R337

Witdrift

Sondags

Vogel

EF

R75

15

Waterford   R400

70

J61

8   *Volkers*

Greystone   *Darlington*   *Darlington Lake Lodge*   **Klipfontein**
                 Dam

23

41

Salt Pan's Nek

Sundays   *Kabouga Guesthouse*

Addo Elephant National Park

Wolwefontein

J62   *Kleinpoort*   *Mvubu*

Blaauwbosch Private   35
Game Reserve

Bontrug

Glenconnor   **Kirkwood**

J63   17

11   *Suday's River Citrus Co.*   R336   32

18   *Kariega*   *Daniel Cheetah*   *Sunland*
                  Breeding Research   19   *Bluecliff*   Su

Cockscomb   53
1758m

EG

30

Groenfal
Wilderness
NR

25

Kwazunga

Groendal Wilderness
Nature Reserve

Elands   **EH**

Gonjah (4x4)   **Stinkhoutberg**
               Nature Reserve   *Swartkops*   **Blindekloof**

Demistkraal   *Rooikrans Campsite*   **J64**

R331   **Uitenhage**

...kraal   **Patensie**   13   **Kleinrivier**   *Offcamber*   **Despatch**
                                                   Adventures 4x4
Fairview   R334
Philip Tunnel   *Sarah Baartman's Grave*   16   **KwaNobuhle**
Hankey   R368

24

25°00'E

37   38   18   39
            Witteklip/N2   *Port Elizabeth*

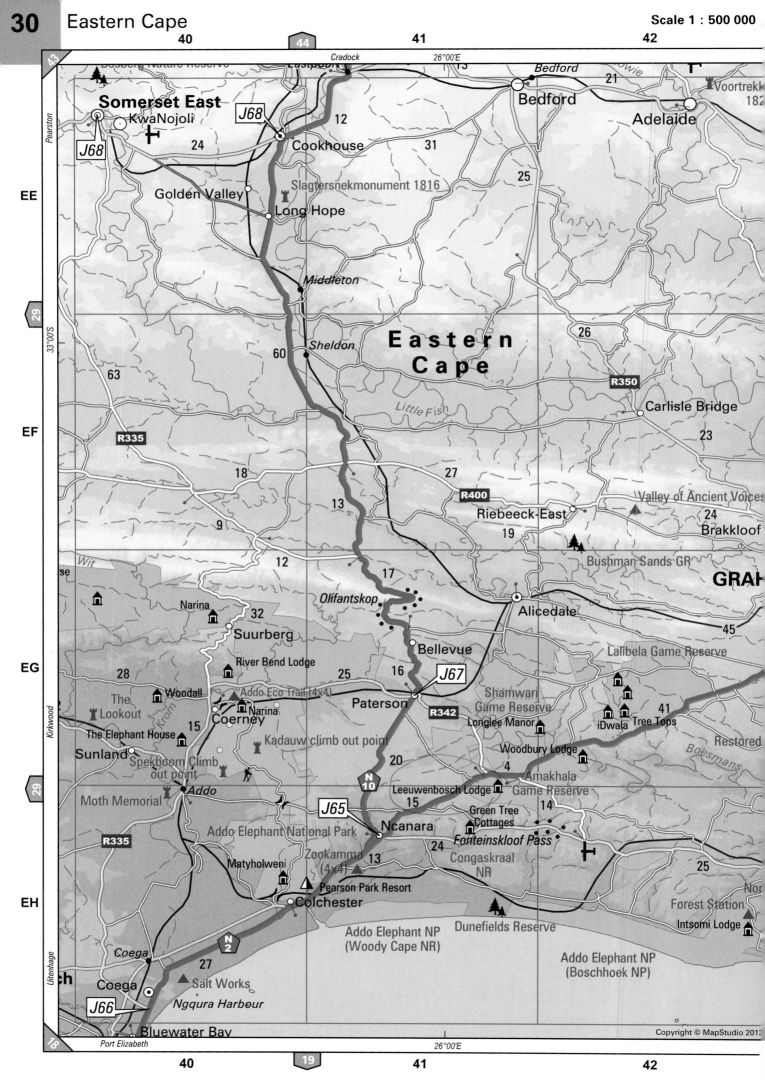

40   44   41   42

Cradock

Bosberg Nature Reserve

Somerset East

KwaNojoli

J68

J68

24

Cookhouse

12

Bedford

Bedford

21

Voortrekke

Adelaide

182

Golden Valley

Long Hope

Slagtersnekmonument 1816

31

25

EE

Middleton

E a s t e r n
C a p e

26

29

33°00'S

60

Sheldon

63

Little Fish

R350

Carlisle Bridge

EF

R335

18

27

R400

13

Riebeeck-East

23

9

19

Valley of Ancient Voices

24

Brakkloof

12

Bushman Sands GR

GRAH

17

Olifantskop

Narina

32

Suurberg

Alicedale

45

River Bend Lodge

Bellevue

Lalibela Game Reserve

EG

28

Woodall

25

16

J67

The Lookout

Addo Eco Trail (4x4)

Paterson

Shamwari
Game Reserve

Longlee Manor

iDwala

Tree Tops

41

Narina

Coerney

R342

The Elephant House

15

Kadauw climb out point

Woodbury Lodge

Sunland

Spekboom Climb
out point

20

4

Restored

Boesmans

29

Moth Memorial

Addo

15

Leeuwenbosch Lodge

Amakhala
Game Reserve

14

R335

J65

Ncanara

Green Tree
Cottages

Addo Elephant National Park

Zookamma
(4x4)

13

24

Fonteinskloof Pass

Congaskraal
NR

25

Matyholweni

Pearson Park Resort

EH

Colchester

Addo Elephant NP
(Woody Cape NR)

Dunefields Reserve

Forest Station

Intsomi Lodge

Coega

N2

Addo Elephant NP
(Boschhoek NP)

Coega

27

Salt Works

Ngqura Harbour

J66

Bluewater Bay

Port Elizabeth

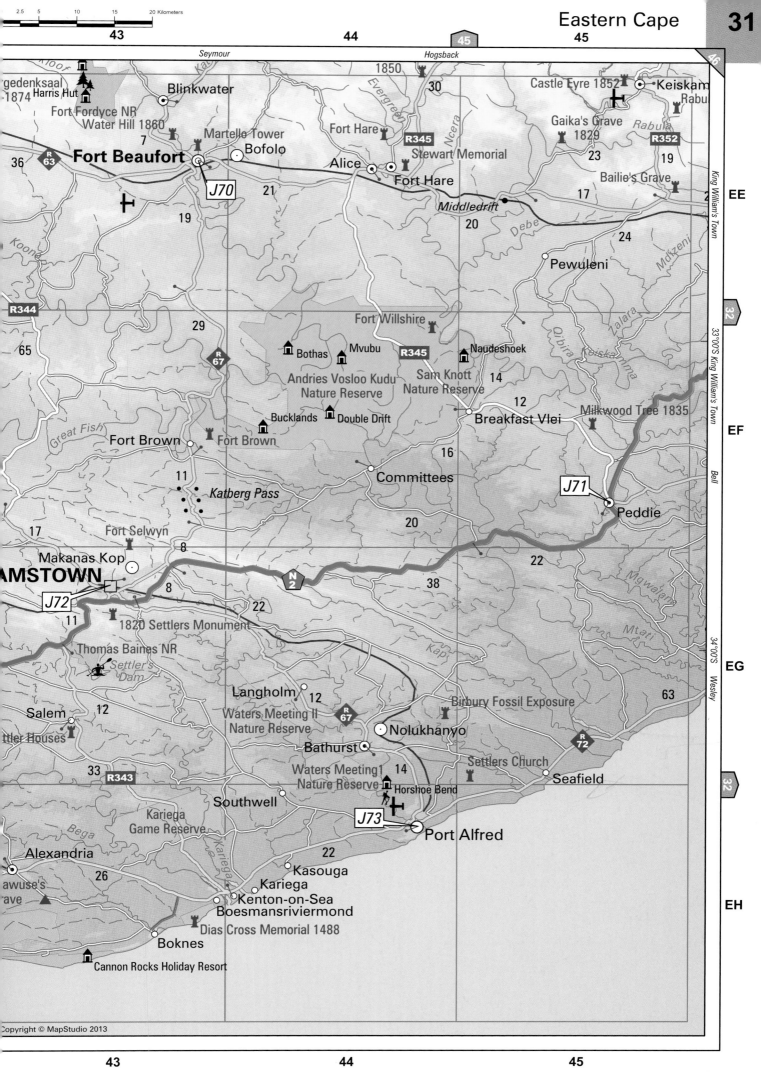

2.5 5   10   15   20 Kilometers

43   **44**   45   **45**

Seymour   Hogsback

gedenksaal 1874   Harris Hut   Blinkwater   1850   30   Castle Eyre 1852   Keiskam
Fort Fordyce NR   Rabu
Water Hill 1860   Martello Tower   Fort Hare   Gaika's Grave   Rabula
7   **Fort Beaufort**   Bofolo   R345   1829   R352
36   R63   Alice   Stewart Memorial   23   Bailie's Grave   19
                 J70   21   Fort Hare   17   EE
           19   Middledrift   20   24
                                              Pewuleni

R344   29   Fort Willshire
65   R67   Bothas   Mvubu   R345   Naudeshoek   14   Milkwood Tree 1835   EF
                 Andries Vosloo Kudu   Sam Knott   12
                 Nature Reserve   Nature Reserve   Breakfast Vlei
                 Bucklands Double Drift
Fort Brown Fort Brown   16   J71
11   Peddie
Katberg Pass   Committees
17   Fort Selwyn   20
8   Makanas Kop   22   EG
AMSTOWN   N2   38
J72   8   22   1820 Settlers Monument   Birbury Fossil Exposure   63
11   Thomas Baines NR   R72
Settler's Dam
Salem   12   Langholm   12   Nolukhanyo   Settlers Church
tler Houses   Waters Meeting II   R67   Bathurst   Seafield   32
33   R343   Nature Reserve   14   Horshoe Bend
Southwell   Waters Meeting I   J73
Kariega   Nature Reserve   Port Alfred
Game Reserve
Alexandria   22   Kasouga   EH
26   Kariega
awuse's   Kenton-on-Sea
rave   Boesmansriviermond
Boknes   Dias Cross Memorial 1488
Cannon Rocks Holiday Resort

43   **44**   **45**

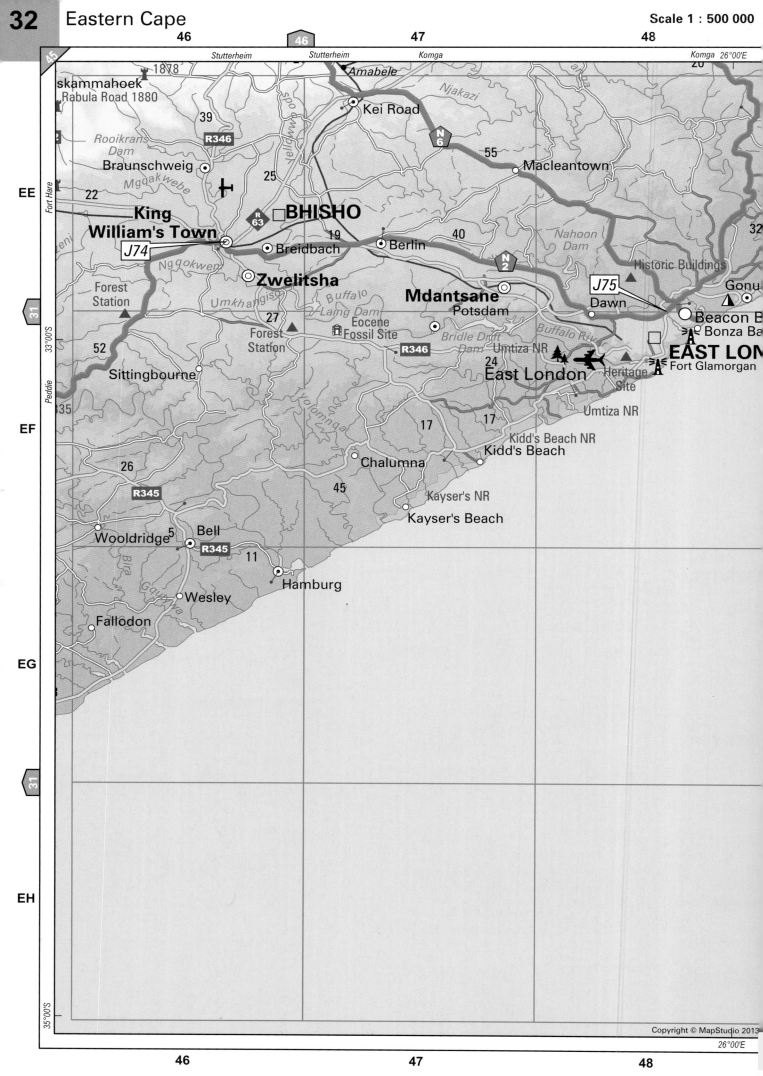

46   46   47   48

Stutterheim   Stutterheim   Komga   Komga 26°00'E

skammahoek
Rabula Road 1880
1878
39
Rooikrans Dam
Braunschweig
22
Mgqakwebe

EE

Fort Hare

King William's Town
J74
R346
R 63
□ **BHISHO**
25
19
Breidbach
Ngqokwen
Berlin
40
Nahoon Dam

◎ **Zwelitsha**
Umkhangiso
Buffalo
Laing Dam

Forest Station
52
27
Forest Station
Eocene Fossil Site
R346
Bridle Drift Dam
Buffalo River

Mdantsane
Potsdam

N2

J75
Dawn
Historic Buildings
Gonu

Beacon B
Bonza Ba
EAST LON
Fort Glamorgan

31
33°00'S

Peddie
35
Sittingbourne
24
Umtiza NR
East London
Heritage Site
Umtiza NR

EF

26
17
17
R345
Chalumna
Kidd's Beach NR
Kidd's Beach
45
Kayser's NR
Wooldridge 5
Bell
R345
Kayser's Beach
11
Bira
Gqunu
Hamburg
Wesley
Fallodon

EG

EH

31
35°00'S

26°00'E

46   47   48

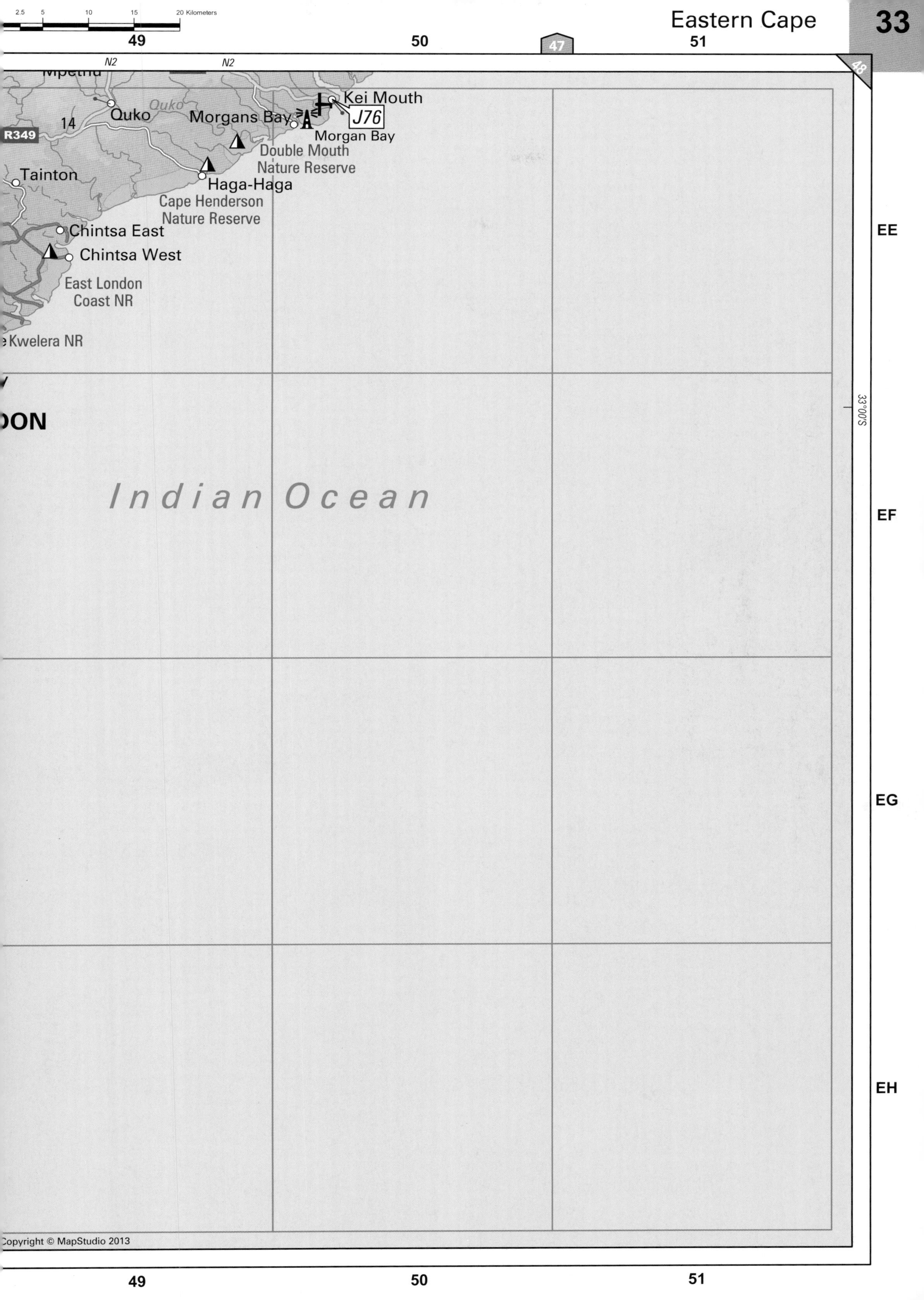

2.5   5   10   15   20 Kilometers

Mpethu

N2   N2

Quko

Quko

Morgans Bay

Kei Mouth

J76

14

R349

Morgan Bay

Double Mouth
Nature Reserve

Tainton

Haga-Haga

Cape Henderson
Nature Reserve

Chintsa East

Chintsa West

East London
Coast NR

e Kwelera NR

DON

33°0'0"S

Indian Ocean

EE

EF

EG

EH

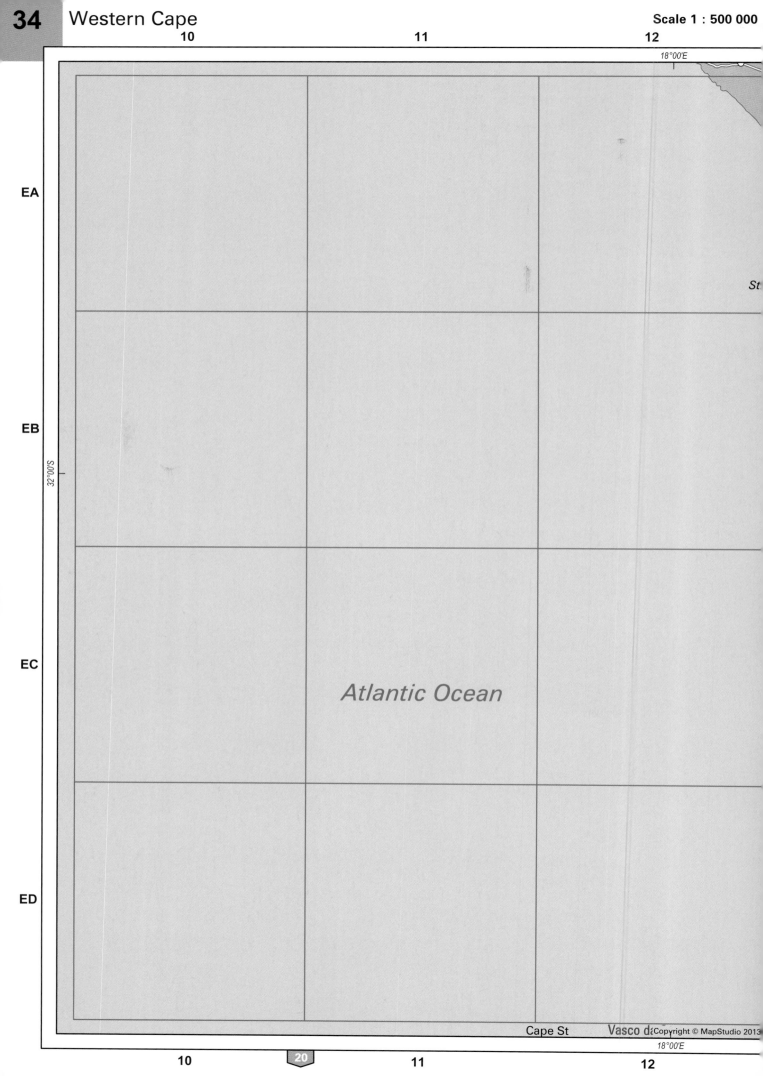

2.5 5 10 15 20 Kilometers

13 14 15

Bitterfontein
Grootdrif

Koekenaap
Koekenaap
Bushman Painting
Lutzville
Melkboomsdrift Lodge
Lutzville
Vleermuisklip 1661
Lutzville
23
Saldanha/Sishen Railway Bridge
Lossand
R362
Olifants
27
31
R363
Vredendal
Stoumann's
Vredendal
17
Spruitdrif
R362
22
22

Maskamsig
R27
49
Vanrhijn & Latsky Radio Museum
Vanrhynsdorp
J77
Cactus Nursery
Anglo-Boer War Fort
25
Urionskraal

EA

33°00'S
36

Estuary Boat Trips
Papendorp
Strandfontein
dfontein Beach
Bamboesbaai
Doringbaai
Grave of Richard Freyer's Wife
59

Klawer
Olives
Rock Art Tours
Klawer
J78
Stellar
Kleipan
Trawal
Trawal
Olifants River Irrigation Scheme
15
N7

EB

1 Lamberts Bay Hotel (EG 79)
2 Lambertsbaai Campsite (EG 79)
3 River Lodge Guesthouse (EF 80)
  Vredendal Hotel (EF 80)
  Voorsorg Guesthouse (EF 80)
  Tharrakamma Guesthouse (EF 80)
4 Clanwilliam Hotel (EG 80)
  Elephant River Guesthouse (EG 80)
  Clanwilliam Lodge (EG 80)

47

Heerenlogement Cave
Heerenlogement

Ratelfontein

Bulshoek Barrage
Rondeberg Resort
38

Olifants

Steenrug (4x4)

Diamond Diving Boats
Panorama Park
Panorama Park Trail (4x4)
Bird "Island"
Lambert's Bay
Annual Crayfish Festival
6
The Dunes Trail (4x4)
16
Desert Hiking Trail
Jakkals
Whale Bone House
27
Wolfhuis
10
Leipoldtville
Kreefbaai
Wadrif Salt Pan
Eland
Elands Bay Hotel
Crayfish Industry
Large Wild Olive Grove
Elandsbaai NR
Elandsbaai
J81
28
Verlorevlei

Graafwater Hotel
R364
9
Graafwater
Jakkals
14
R365
Sandberg
27
Lang
Lambertshoek

Guided Rooibosch Tours
J79
29
Clanwilliam
Clanwilliam Dam
Old Gaol (Jail) Museum
Kle
52
Die Kleine Schuur
J80
La Rhyn
Gekko

EC

36

Redelinghuys
Jakkalskloof (4x4)
Castle Trail
26
Noordkuil
Historic Ammunition Store, Ruins & San Art
18
Verlorevlei
Paleisheuwel
Sewefontein
Scenic Paleisheuwel Drive
Het Kruis
Ro

ED

J
Citr

Rocherpan Nature Reserve
28
Papkuil
Dwarskersbos
warskersbos
Copyright © MapStudio 2013

Kruismans
Droëryskloof
Piekenierskloof

Citrusdal
Citrusdal

Piketberg Piketberg

13 14 21 15

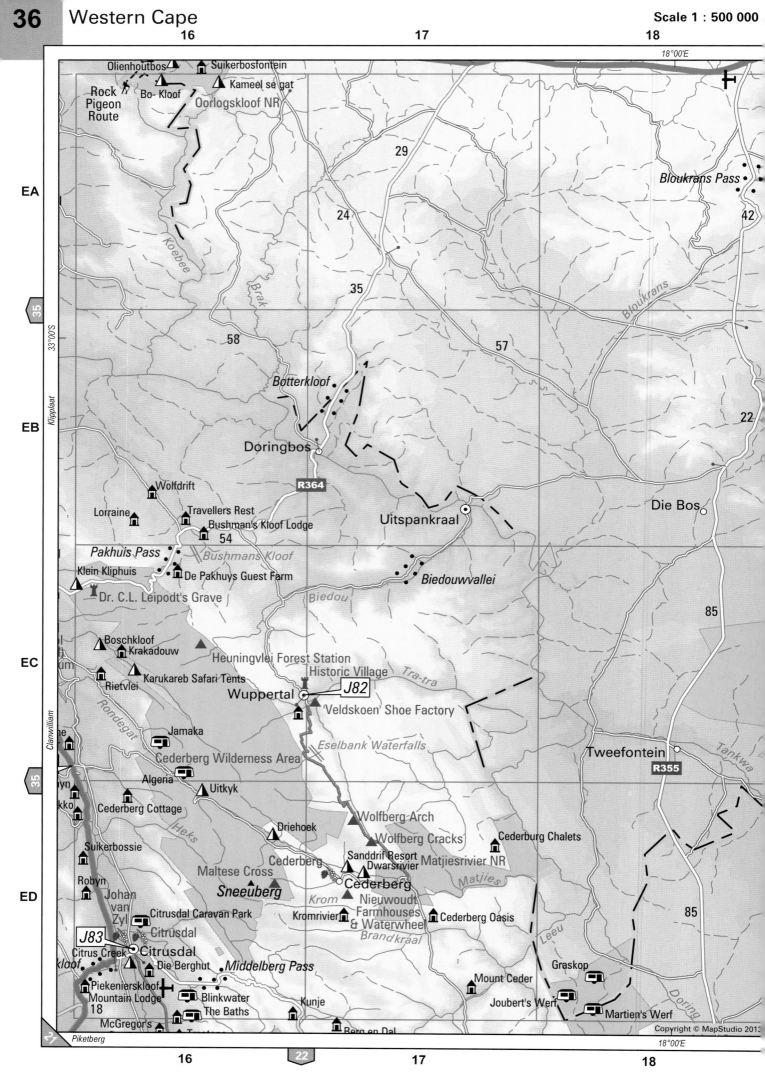

18°00'E

16   **17**   **18**

Olienhoutbos
Suikerbosfontein
Rock Pigeon Route
Bo- Kloof
Kameel se gat
Oorlogskloof NR

29

24

EA

33°00'S

Bloukrans Pass

42

35

Koebee
Brak

35

58

57

22

Botterkloof

EB

Bloukrans

Doringbos

R364

Uitspankraal

Die Bos

Wolfdrift

Klipplaat

Lorraine
Travellers Rest
Bushman's Kloof Lodge
54

Pakhuis Pass
Bushmans Kloof
Klein Kliphuis
De Pakhuys Guest Farm
Dr. C.L. Leipodt's Grave

Biedou
Biedouwvallei

85

Boschkloof
Krakadouw

Heuningvlei Forest Station
Historic Village
Tra-tra

EC

Clanwilliam

Rietvlei
Karukareb Safari Tents

Wuppertal   J82
'Veldskoen' Shoe Factory

Tweefontein
R355

Tankwa

Rondegat

Jamaka
Cederberg Wilderness Area
Eselbank Waterfalls

35

Heks

Algeria
Uitkyk

ED

kko
Cederberg Cottage

Driehoek
Wolfberg Arch
Wolfberg Cracks
Cederburg Chalets

Suikerbossie
Maltese Cross
Cederberg
Sanddrif Resort
Dwarsrivier
Matjiesrivier NR

Matjies

Robyn
Sneeuberg
Cederberg
Nieuwoudt Farmhouses & Waterwheel
Cederberg Oasis

85

Johan van Zyl
Krom
Kromrivier
Brandkraal

Citrusdal Caravan Park
Citrusdal

J83
Citrus Creek
Citrusdal
Die Berghut
Middelberg Pass

Leeu

Graskop

Mount Ceder

Doring

Piekenierskloof Mountain Lodge
18
Blinkwater
The Baths
McGregor's
Kunje

Joubert's Werf
Martien's Werf

Piketberg
Berg en Dal

Copyright © MapStudio 2013

18°00'E

16   **22**   **17**   **18**

21

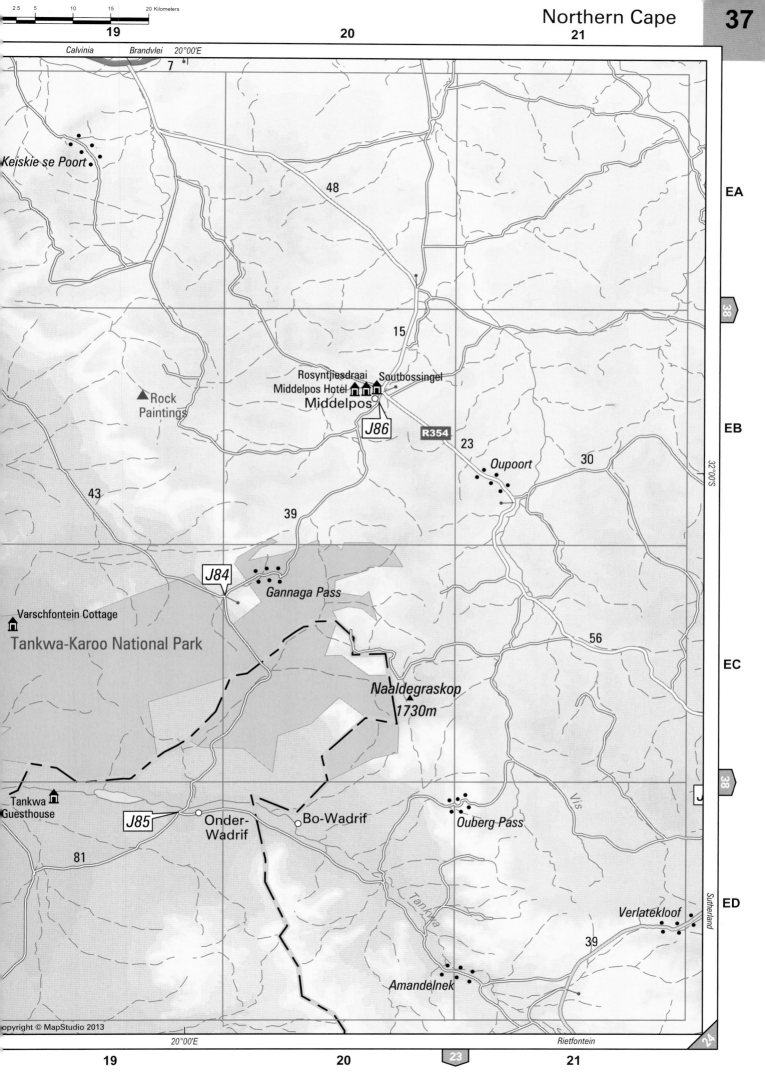

2.5 5 10 15 20 Kilometers

19 20 **21**

Calvinia   Brandvlei   20°00'E

7

Keiskie se Poort

48

15

EA

38

Rosyntjiesdraai   Soutbossingel
Middelpos Hotel

Middelpos

J86   R354   23

Oupoort   30

Rock
Paintings

EB

32°00'S

43

39

J84

Gannaga Pass

Varschfontein Cottage

Tankwa-Karoo National Park

56

Naaldegraskop
1730m

EC

38

Tankwa
Guesthouse

J85   Onder-
Wadrif   Bo-Wadrif   Ouberg Pass

Vis

J

81

ED

Verlatekloof   Sutherland

Tankwa

39

Amandelnek

20°00'E   Rietfontein

23

24

19 20 **21**

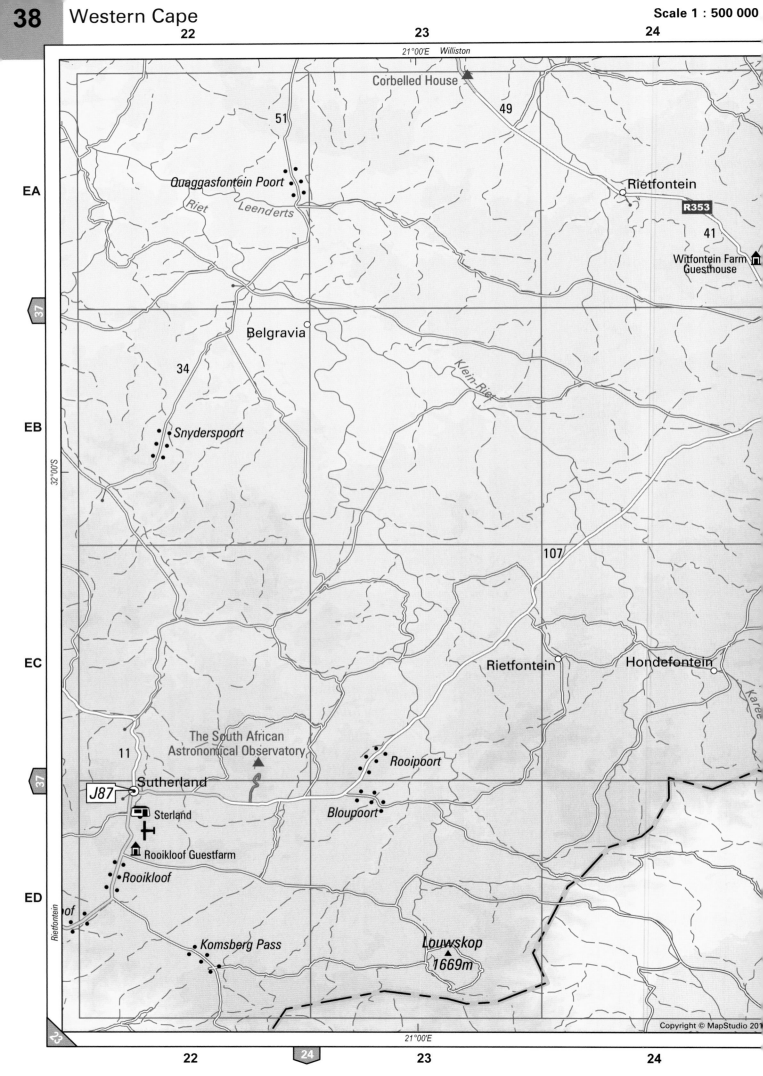

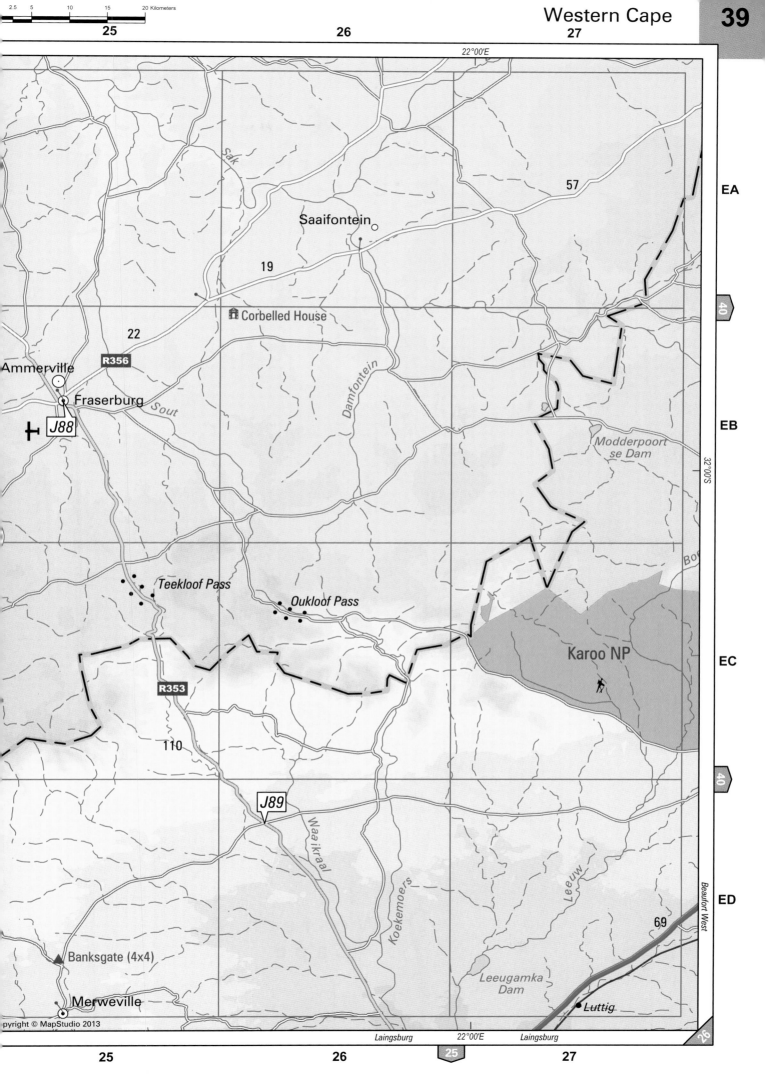

2.5 5 10 15 20 Kilometers

25

26

27

22°00'E

EA

57

Saaifontein

19

40

🏠 Corbelled House

22

R356

Ammerville

Fraserburg

Sout

J88

Damfontein

EB

Modderpoort se Dam

32°00'S

Teekloof Pass

Oukloof Pass

Karoo NP

EC

R353

110

J89

Waaikraal

Koekemoers

Leeuw

40

ED

Beaufort West

69

▲ Banksgate (4x4)

Merweville

Leeugamka Dam

• Luttig

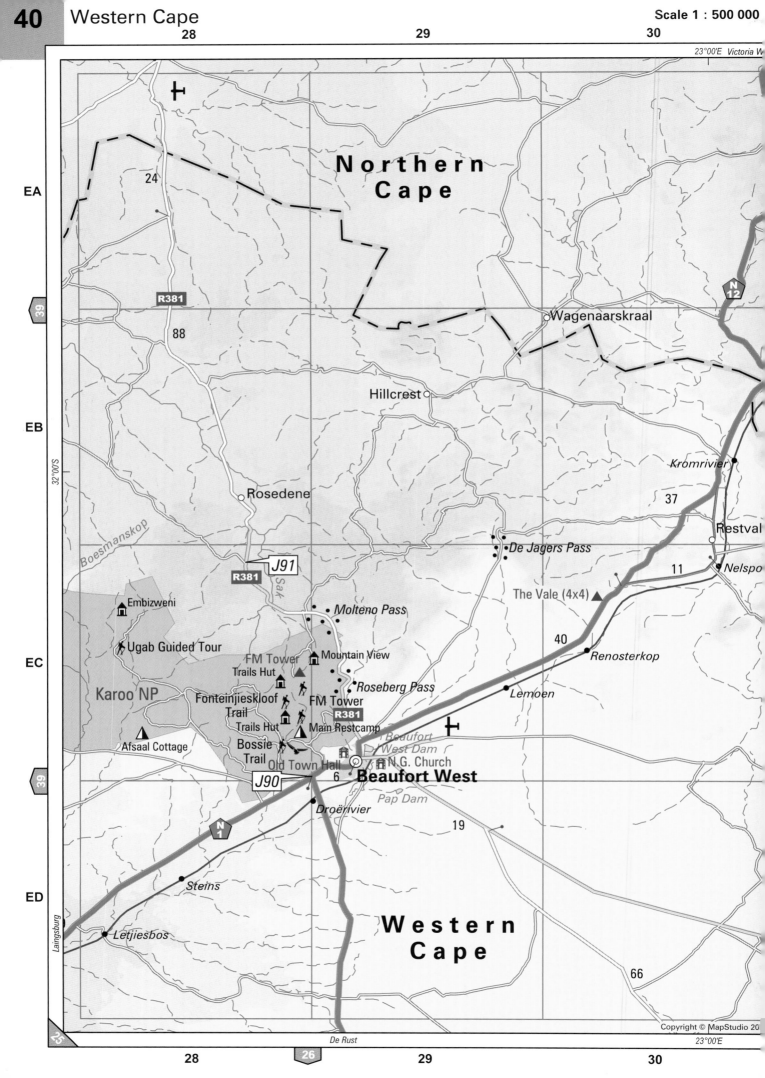

Northern Cape

24

R381

88

Hillcrest ○

Wagenaarskraal ○

Rosedene ○

Boesmanskop

Kromrivier

37

Restval ○

De Jagers Pass

Nelspo

J91

Sak

R381

11

▲ Embizweni

The Vale (4x4) ▲

40

Molteno Pass

Renosterkop

Ugab Guided Tour

FM Tower

Mountain View

Trails Hut ▲

Lemoen

Karoo NP

Fonteinjieskloof Trail

Roseberg Pass

FM Tower

Trails Hut

R381

▲ Main Restcamp

Beaufort West Dam

△ Afsaal Cottage

Bossie Trail

Old Town Hall

N.G. Church

6   **Beaufort West**

J90

Pap Dam

Droërivier

19

Laingsburg

N1

● _Steins_

● _Letjiesbos_

Western Cape

66

32°00'S

39

39

EA

EB

EC

ED

De Rust

25

26

28

29

30

23°00'E _Victoria W_

23°00'E

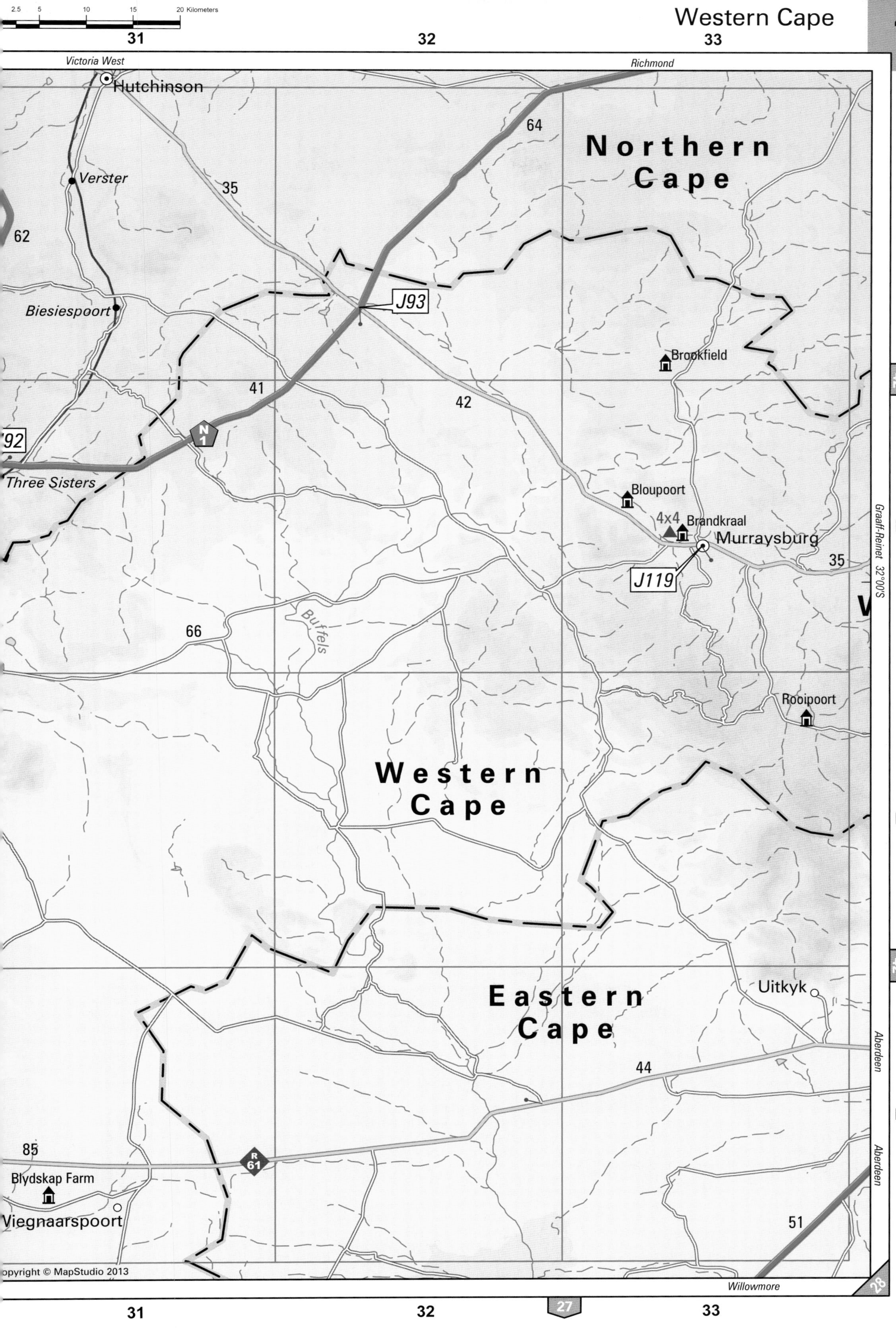

2.5 5   10   15   20 Kilometers

31   **32**   **33**

Victoria West   Richmond

⊙ Hutchinson

64

Verster

N o r t h e r n
C a p e

35

62

J93

Biesiespoort ●

Brookfield

41

42

92

N
1

EA

42

Three Sisters

Bloupoort

4x4 Brandkraal

⊙ Murraysburg

EB

J119

35

66

Buffels

Rooipoort

W e s t e r n
C a p e

EC

42

E a s t e r n
C a p e

Uitkyk ○

44

ED

85

Aberdeen

R
61

Blydskap Farm

51

Viegnaarspoort ○

Willowmore

31   **32**   27   **33**

Graaff-Reinet 32°00'S

28

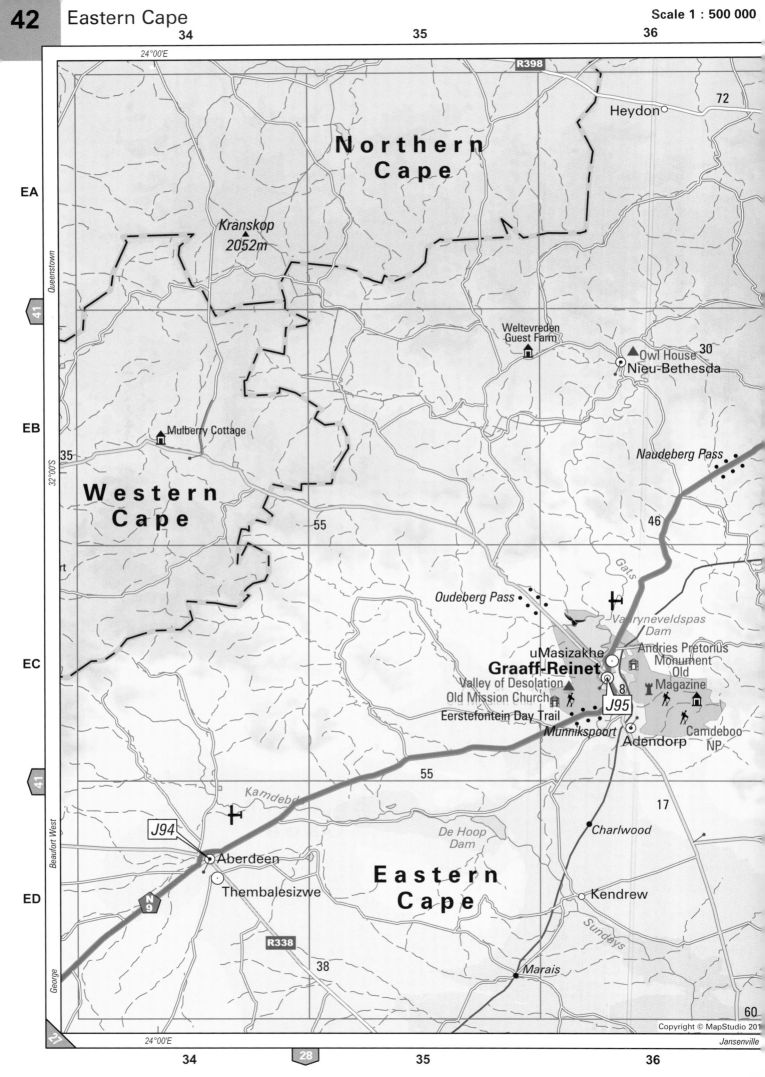

34   35   36

EA

EB

EC

ED

41

41

R398

72

Heydon

**N o r t h e r n
C a p e**

24°00'E

Kranskop
2052m

Weltevreden
Guest Farm

Owl House
Nieu-Bethesda

30

Mulberry Cottage

Naudeberg Pass

32°00'S

35

**W e s t e r n
C a p e**

55

46

Gats

Oudeberg Pass

Vanryneveldspas
Dam

uMasizakhe
Graaff-Reinet

Andries Pretorius
Monument
Old
Magazine

Valley of Desolation

Old Mission Church

J95

8

Eerstefontein Day Trail

Munnikspoort

Adendorp

Camdeboo
NP

Camdeboo
NP

55

17

Kamdeb

Charlwood

J94

De Hoop
Dam

Beaufort West

Aberdeen

**E a s t e r n
C a p e**

Thembalesizwe

Kendrew

N9

Sundays

R338

38

Marais

60

George

24°00'E

Jansenville

Queenstown

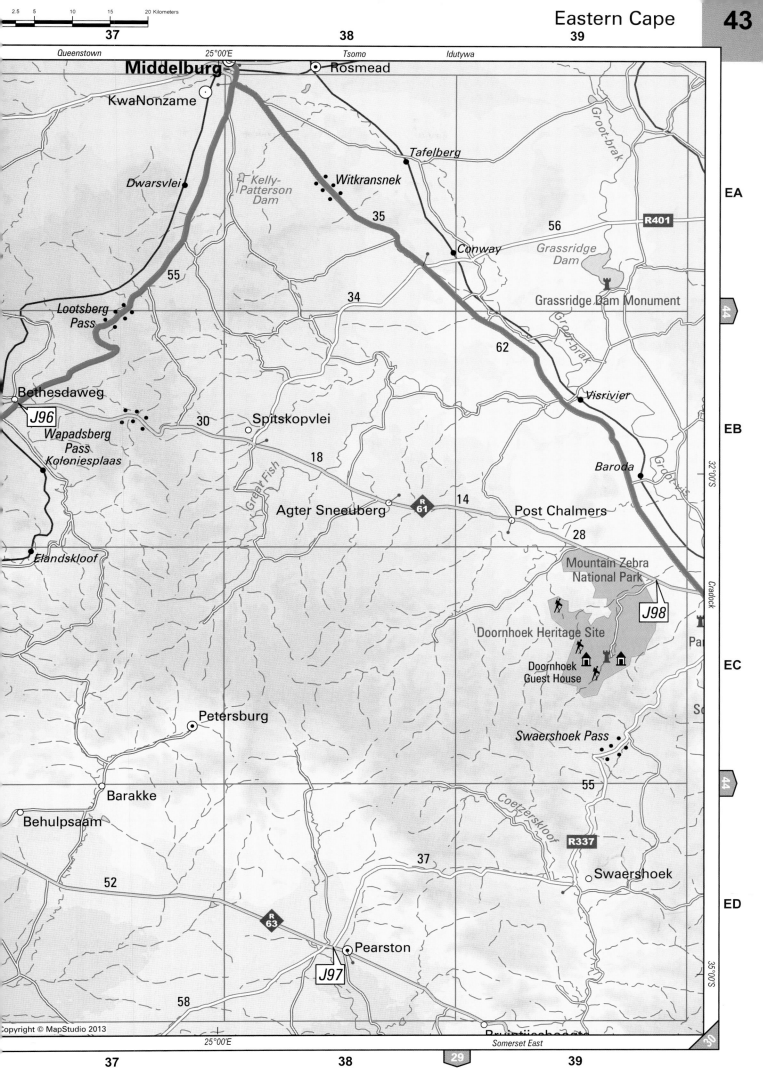

2.5 5   10   15   20 Kilometers

37   38   39

Queenstown   25°00'E   Tsomo   Idutywa

Middelburg   Rosmead

KwaNonzame

Tafelberg

Dwarsvlei   Witkransnek

Kelly-
Patterson
Dam   35   56   R401

Conway   Grassridge
Dam

55   Grassridge Dam Monument

Lootsberg
Pass   34   62

Visrivier

Bethesdaweg

J96   30   Spitskopvlei   Baroda

Wapadsberg
Pass
Koloniesplaas   18

Great Fish   14   Post Chalmers

Agter Sneeuberg   R61   28

Elandskloof   Mountain Zebra
National Park

J98

Doornhoek Heritage Site

Doornhoek
Guest House

Petersburg   Swaershoek Pass

Barakke

Behulpsaam   55

Coetzerskloof

R337

37   Swaershoek

52

R63

Pearston

J97

58

Copyright © MapStudio 2013

25°00'E   Somerset East

37   38   29   39

EA

44

EB   32°00'S

EC   Cradock

ED   35°00'S

36

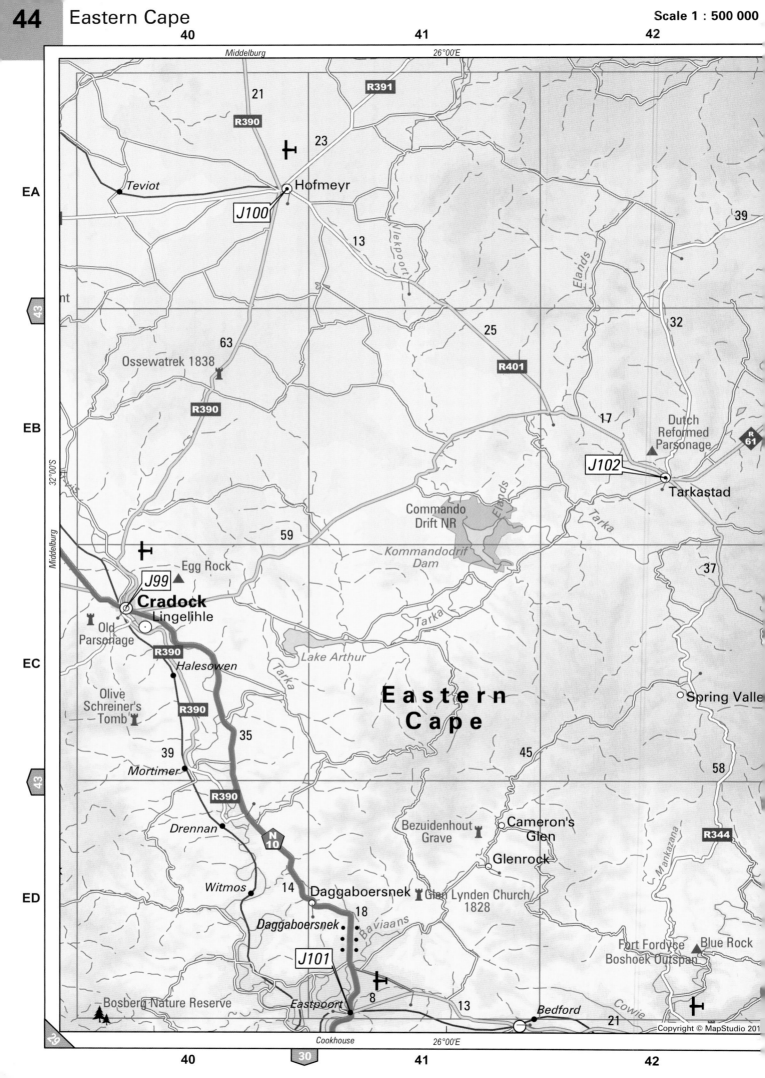

Middelburg

R391

21

R390

23

Teviot

Hofmeyr

J100

39

13

32

25

R401

63

Ossewatrek 1838

Dutch
Reformed
Parsonage

17

R390

J102

Tarkastad

R61

Commando
Drift NR

37

*Kommandodrif
Dam*

59

Egg Rock

J99

Cradock

Lingelihle

Old
Parsonage

Tarka

Lake Arthur

R390

Halesowen

**E a s t e r n
C a p e**

Spring Valle

Olive
Schreiner's
Tomb

R390

35

39

45

58

Mortimer

R390

Drennan

Bezuidenhout
Grave

**Cameron's
Glen**

R344

N10

Glenrock

Witmos

14

Daggaboersnek

Glen Lynden Church
1828

Daggaboersnek

18

Baviaans

J101

Fort Fordyce
Boshoek Outspan

Blue Rock

8

Bosberg Nature Reserve

Eastpoort

13

Bedford

21

Cowie

Middelburg 26°00'E

32°00'S

Niekpoort

Elands

Elands

Tarka

Mankazana

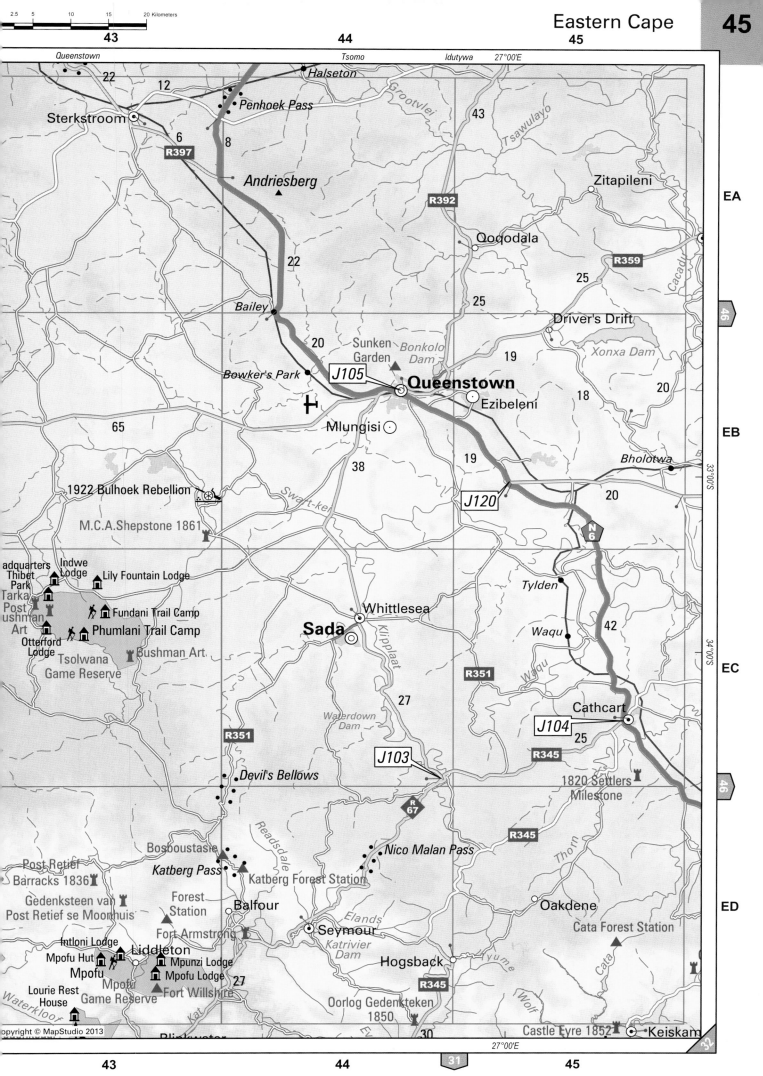

2.5 5   10   15   20 Kilometers

Queenstown   Tsomo   Idutywa   27°00'E

Halseton

22   12   Penhoek Pass

Sterkstroom

6   8

R397

Andriesberg

R392

Zitapileni

Qoqodala   R359

25   Driver's Drift   Xonxa Dam

22   Bailey   Sunken Garden   Bonkolo Dam   19   18   20

20   J105   Queenstown   EB

Bowker's Park   Ezibeleni

Mlungisi   19   Bholotwa

65   38   J120   20

1922 Bulhoek Rebellion   N6

M.C.A.Shepstone 1861

adquarters Thibet Park   Indwe Lodge   Lily Fountain Lodge   Tylden

Tarka Post ushman Art   Fundani Trail Camp   Waqu   42

Phumlani Trail Camp   Whittlesea

Otterford Lodge   Sada   Cathcart

Bushman Art   R351   J104   25

Tsolwana Game Reserve   27

Waterdown Dam   1820 Settlers Milestone

R351   J103

Devil's Bellows   R67   R345

Bosboustasie   Nico Malan Pass

Katberg Pass   R345

Post Retief Barracks 1836   Katberg Forest Station   Thorn

Gedenksteen van Post Retief se Moorhuis   Forest Station   Balfour   Oakdene   Cata Forest Station

Fort Armstrong   Elands   Seymour

Intloni Lodge   Liddleton   Katrivier Dam   Hogsback

Mpofu Hut   Mpunzi Lodge   ED

Mpofu   Mpofu Lodge

Lourie Rest House   Mpofu Game Reserve   Fort Willshire   27   Oorlog Gedenkteken 1850   R345

Waterkloof   Castle Eyre 1852   Keiskam

opyright © MapStudio 2013   Blinkwater   27°00'E

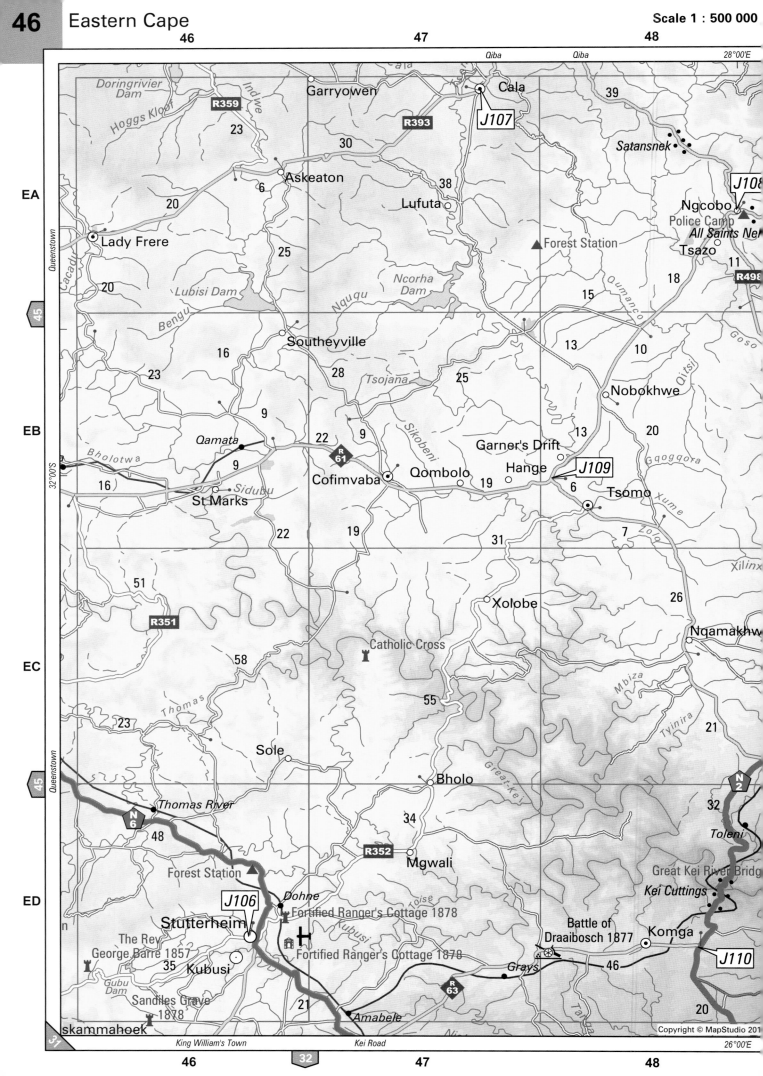

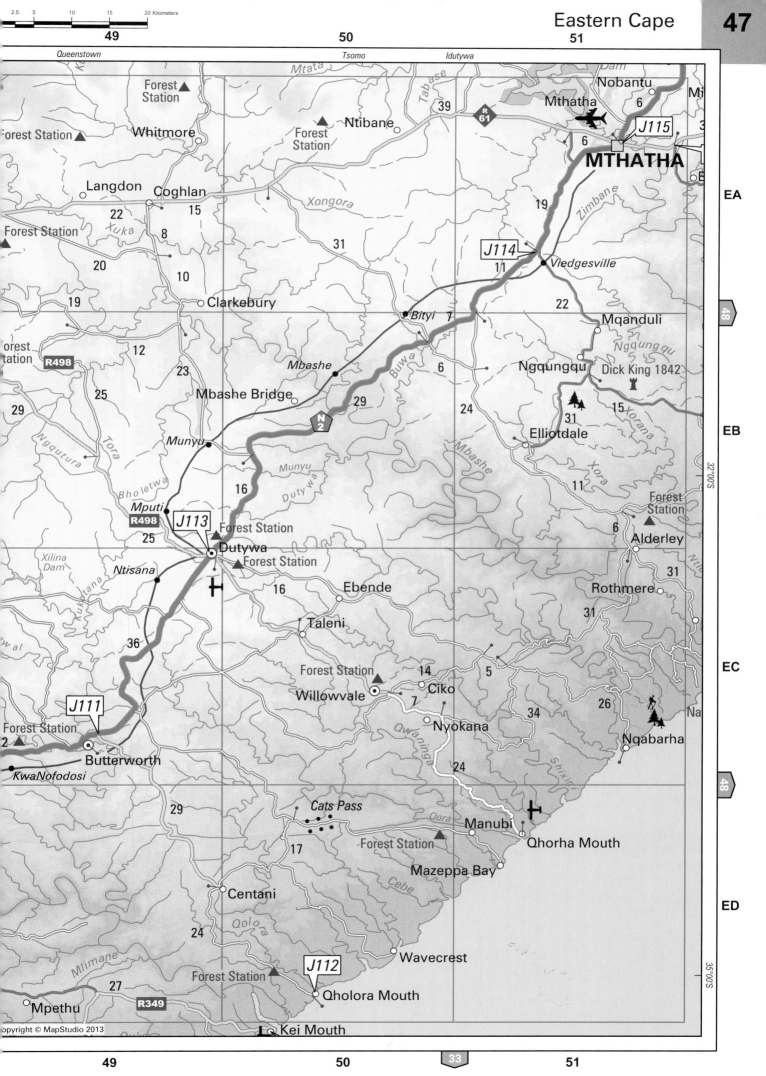

2.5 5 10 15 20 Kilometers
49

Queenstown   Tsomo   Idutywa

Forest Station ▲

Whitmore

Forest Station ▲

Ntibane

Forest Station ▲

39

R 61

Nobantu

Mthatha

6

J115

6

MTHATHA

3

EA

Langdon

Coghlan

22   15

8

20

19

Clarkebury

Forest Station ▲

R498

12

23

25

29

Ngqutura

Tora

Xuka

Xongora

31

Mbashe

Mbashe Bridge

Munyu

Munyu
Dutywa

N 2

29

Bholetwa

Mputi
R498

25

J113

Forest Station ▲

Dutywa

Forest Station ▲

Ntisana

Xilina Dam

Kukqtana

16

Buwa

Bityi   7

6

19

11

J114

Viedgesville

22

Mqanduli

Ngqungqu

Dick King 1842

31

15

Xolana

Elliotdale

11

Xora

Mbashe

24

6

Forest Station ▲

Alderley

31

Rothmere

31

5

14

Ciko

7

Nyokana

34

26

Nqabarha

Na

EB

EC

48

Ebende

Taleni

16

36

J111

Forest Station ▲

2 ▲

Butterworth

KwaNofodosi

Forest Station ▲

Willowvale

Qwaninga

Shixini

Mlimane

29

Cats Pass

17

Centani

24

Qolo

J112

Forest Station ▲

Qholora Mouth

R349

27

Mpethu

Kei Mouth

Qora

Manubi

Qhorha Mouth

Mazeppa Bay

Cebe

Wavecrest

32°00'S

35°00'S

ED

48

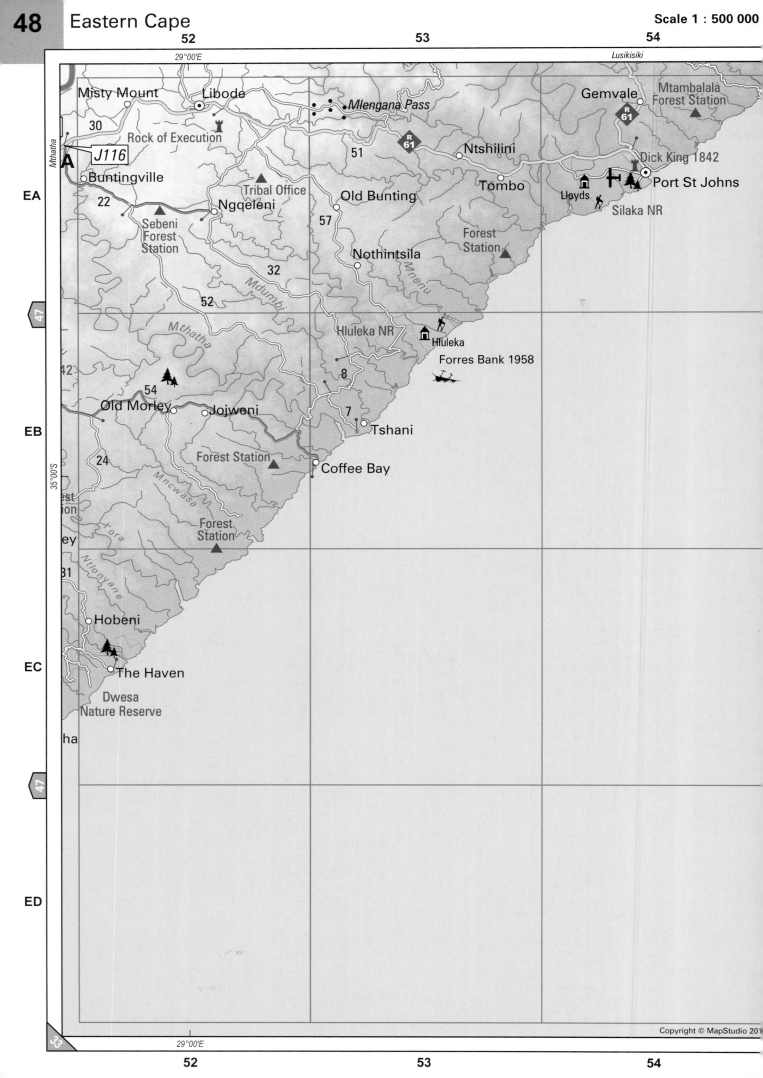

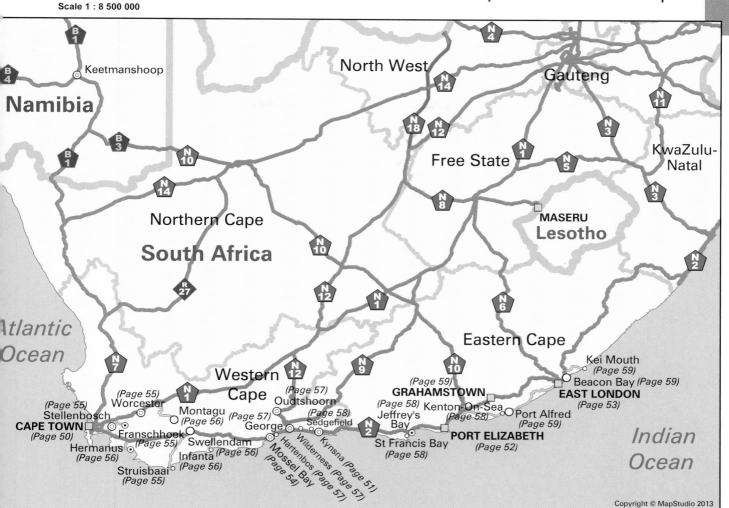

Street Map Legend

Scale 1 : 22 500

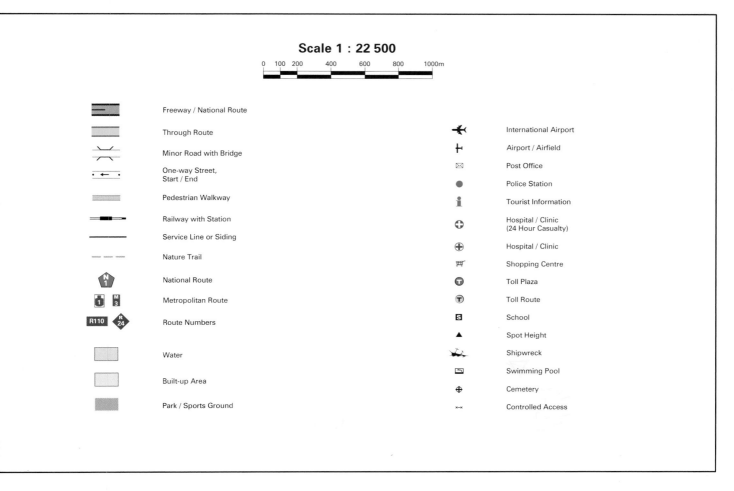

Freeway / National Route	International Airport
Through Route	Airport / Airfield
Minor Road with Bridge	Post Office
One-way Street, Start / End	Police Station
Pedestrian Walkway	Tourist Information
Railway with Station	Hospital / Clinic (24 Hour Casualty)
Service Line or Siding	Hospital / Clinic
Nature Trail	Shopping Centre
National Route	Toll Plaza
Metropolitan Route	Toll Route
Route Numbers	School
	Spot Height
Water	Shipwreck
Built-up Area	Swimming Pool
Park / Sports Ground	Cemetery
	Controlled Access

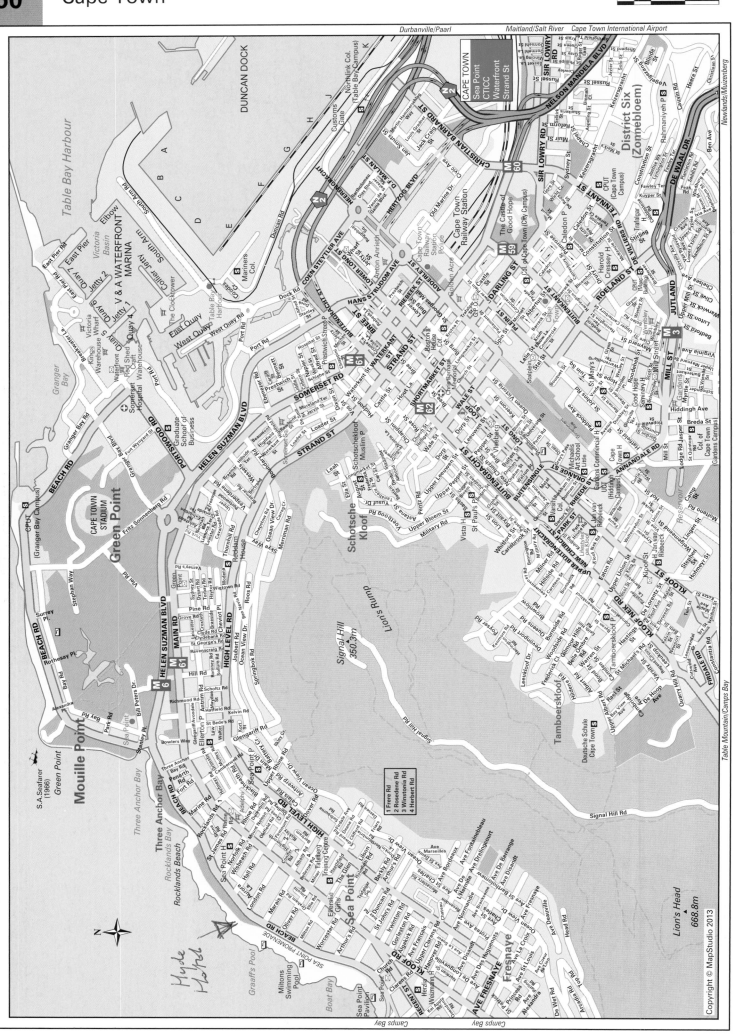

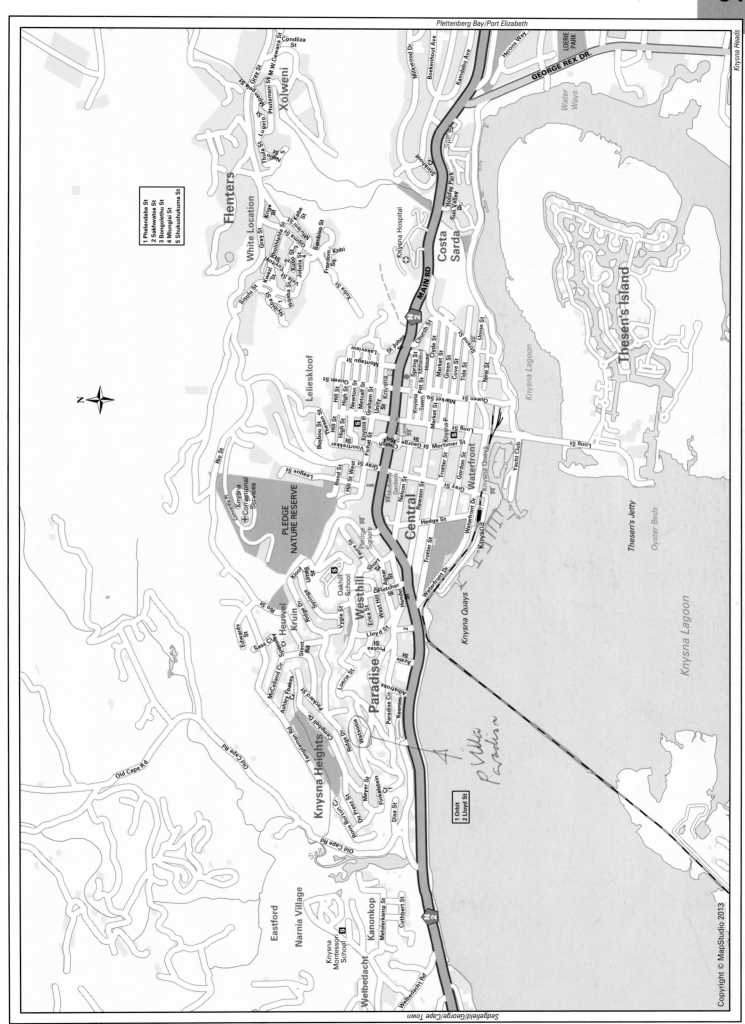

0 100 200   400   600m

GEORGE REX DR.

Knysna Heads

LOERIE PARK

Herons Way

Boekenhout Ave

Millwood Dr.

Kameleo Ave

Sun Valley Dr.

Holiday Park Dr.

Spark

Sinmout

Water Ways

Condilza St

Gray St

W. W. Cewana St

Phutamani St

Mgababa St

Thula St

Lugelo St

Nqiu St 5

Xolweni

Flenters

White Location

1 Phelandaba St
2 Sakhwatsa St
3 Bongolethu St
4 Mlungisi St
5 Shukushukuma St

Kiga St

Grey St

Bholothlahla St

Gllira St

Kobe St

Bambiso St

Toyiyo St

Kwezi St

Kubo St

Jobela St 4

Nyibib's St

Sinabla St

Freedom Kobi Sq.

Xusa St

Sisulu St

Knysna Hospital

Costa Sarda

MAIN RD

N2

Thesen's Island

Knysna Lagoon

St John St

Church St

Clyde St

Union St

Spring St

Pitt St

Millwood House

Market St

Green St

Cove St

Tide St

New St

Lakeview

Montagu St

Queen St

Leliesdoof

Hill St

Hill St

High St

High St

Newton St

Metcalf St

Graham St

Unity St

Knysna Town

Market St

Queen St

Bostou St

Thesen St

Fichat St

Grey St

Church St

St George St

Mortimer St

Long St

Knysna P

Long St

Waterfront

Knysna Quays

Yacht Club

Thesen's Jetty

Oyster Beds

Voortrekker St

Hill St West

Bond St

League St

Rio St

Knysna Correctional Services

PLEDGE NATURE RESERVE

Mulberry Gardens

Nelson St

Rawson St

Trotter St

Gordon St

Gray St

Waterfront Dr.

Knysna

Hedge St

Cooksons Pl

Pledge Square

Fauna Lane

Short St

Kloof St

Uitsig St

Sringa Dr.

Ridge Dr.

Oakhill School

Westhill

West Hill Dr.

Fletcher St

Handel St

Trotter St

Waterfront Dr.

Knysna Quays

Heuwel Kruin

Vygie St

Erica St

Lloyd St

Rio St

Edwards St

Sass Cl.

Spensla

Stent Rd

Protea St

Loerie St

Azalea St

Albatross

1 Orbit
2 Lloyd St

McClelland Cir.

Ashley Foakes Cr.

Packard St

Paradise Cir.

Ketrom St

Paradise

Campbell Dr.

Ridge Dr.

Watsonia

Knysna Heights

Templeman Rd

Old Cape Rd

Meyer St

Du Preez Cr.

Finkelstein Cr.

Disa St

Rooi Ten Loon Cr.

Eastford

Narnia Village

Welbedacht

Kanonkop

Knysna Montessori School

Metelerkamp St

Cuthbert St

Knysna Montessori School S

Old Cape Rd

Salt

Welbedacht Rd

N2

Villa Paradisa

Knysna Lagoon

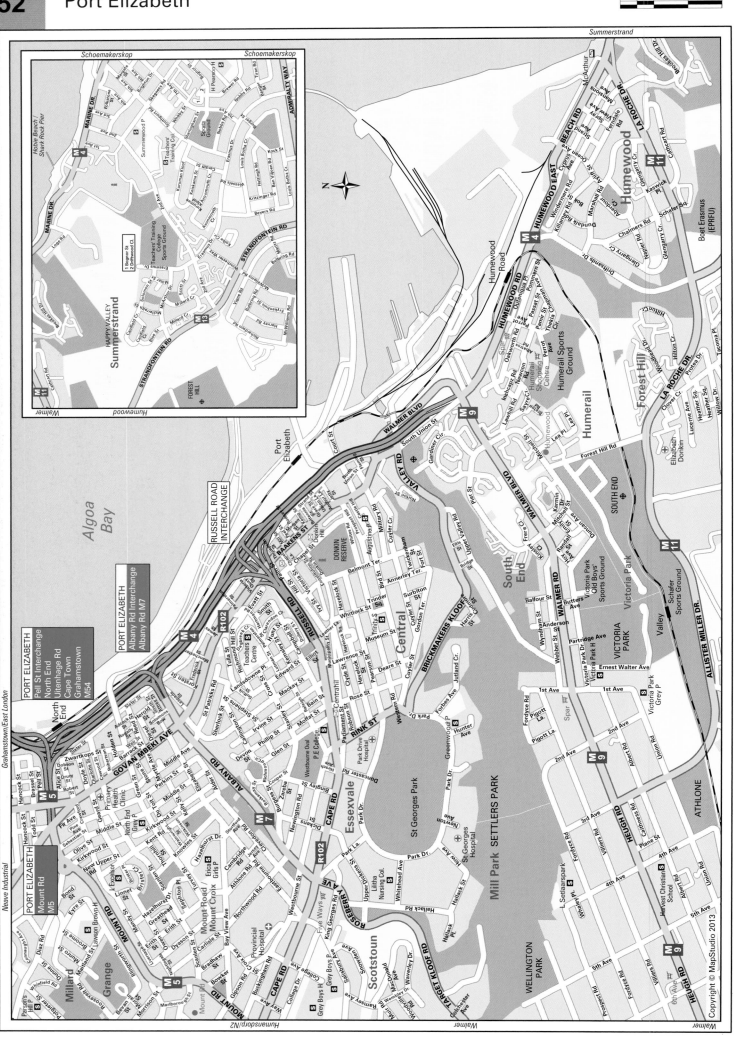

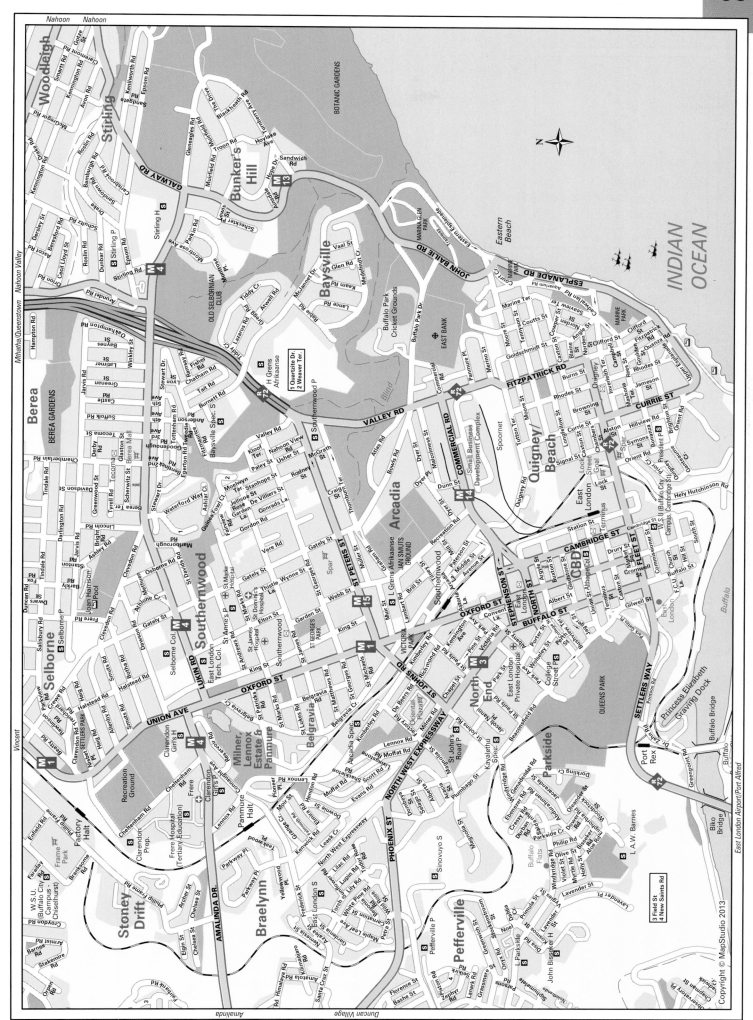

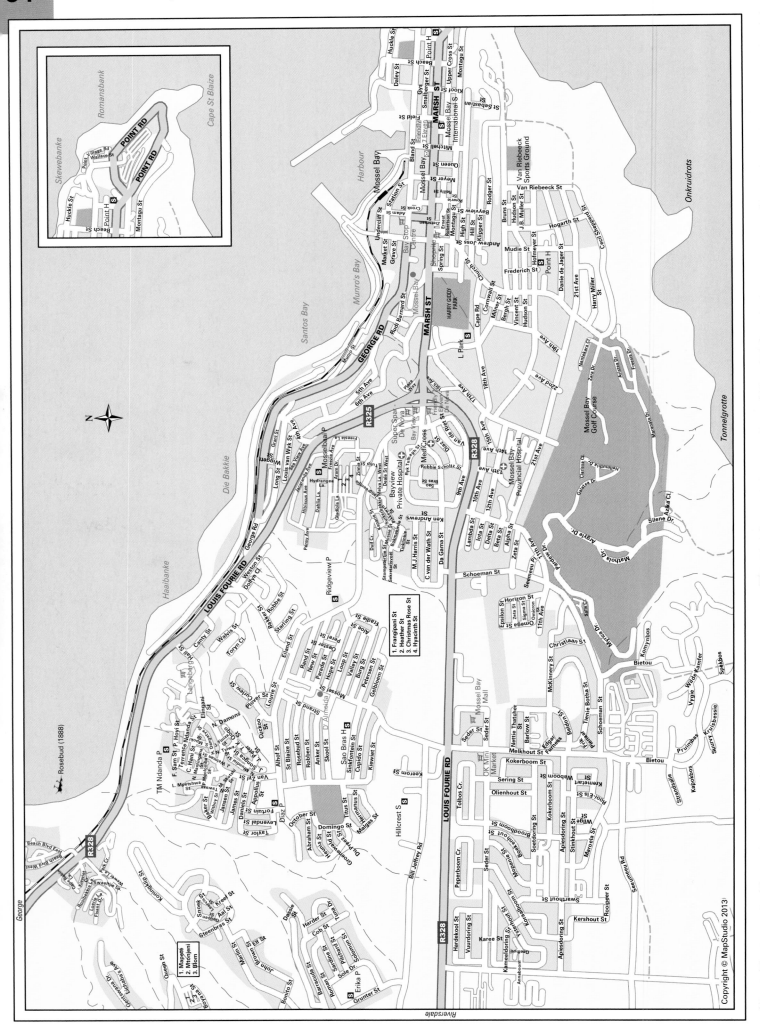

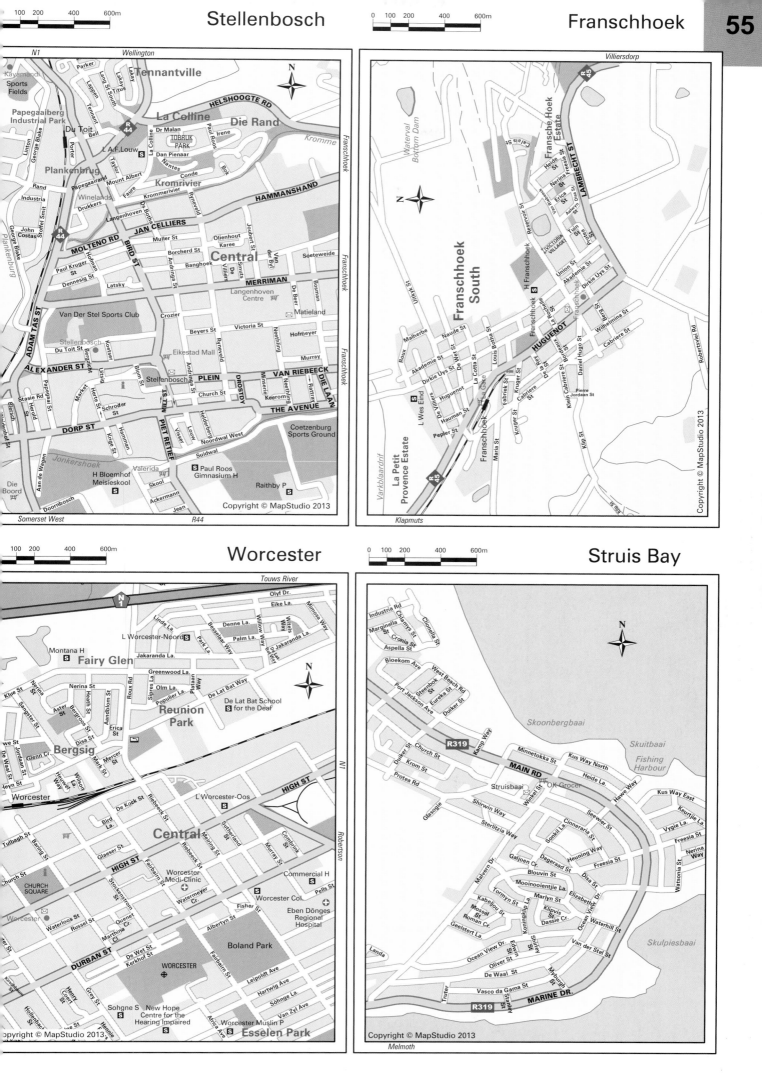

Hermanus

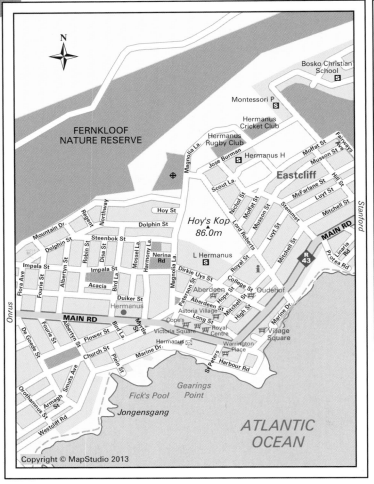

Swellendam

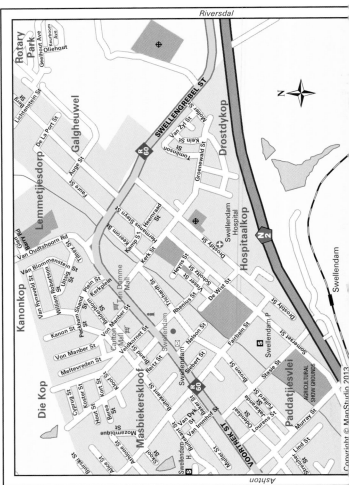

Montagu

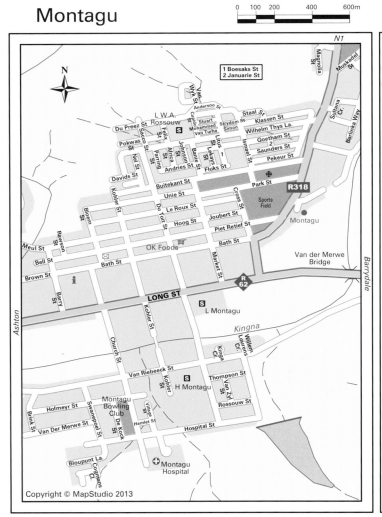

Infanta

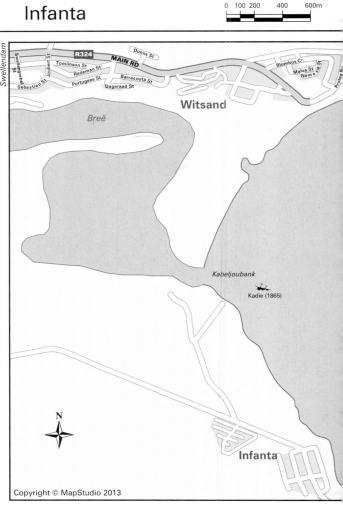

Hartenbos

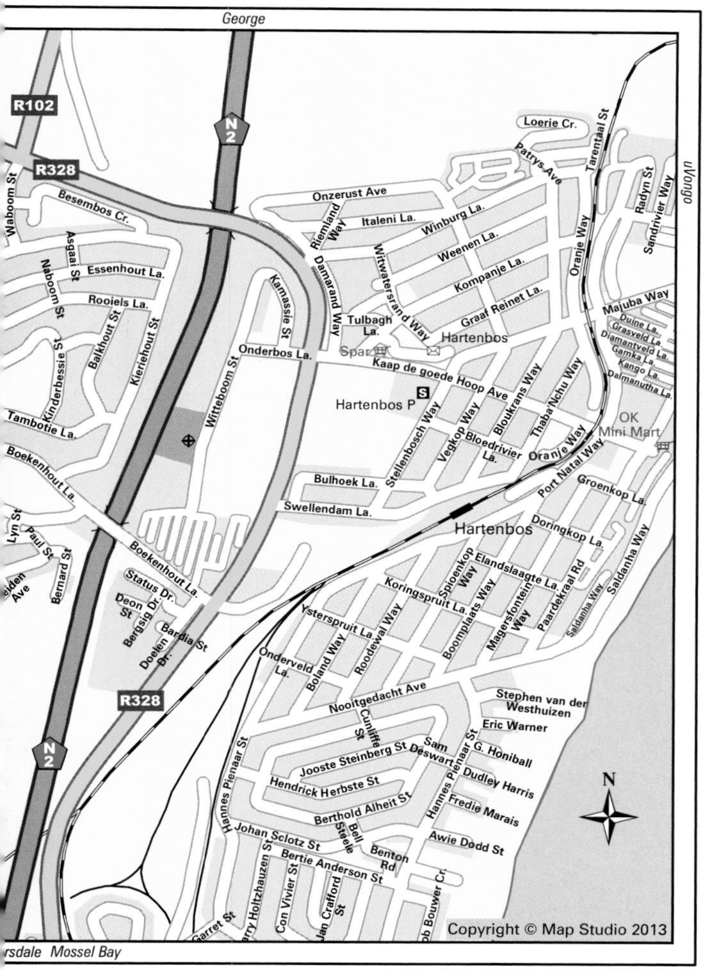

R102
R328
N2
R328
Mosseldale Mossel Bay

Oudtshoorn

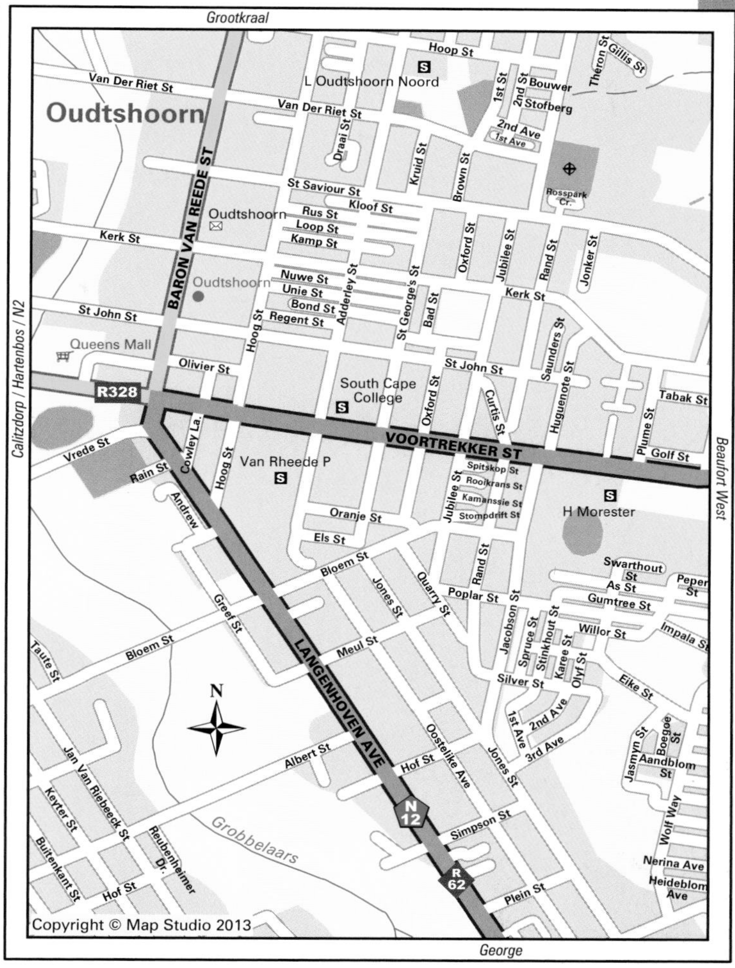

Oudtshoorn
L Oudtshoorn Noord
Queens Mall
R328
VOORTREKKER ST
BARON VAN REEDE ST
LANGENHOVEN AVE
South Cape College
N12
R62
Grobbelaars
George
Beaufort West
Calitzdorp / Hartenbos / N2

George

Heatherlands
SANDF Women's Col.
VAN RIEBEECK GARDEN
George Hospital
Camphers Drift
DAVIDSON RD
C.J. LANGENHOVEN RD
Lamprecht Medi-Clinic
Bodorp
COURTENAY ST
YORK ST
N9
Dormehls Drift
George Central
Woolworths
Market Mall
ALBERT ST
George South
York H
Knysna

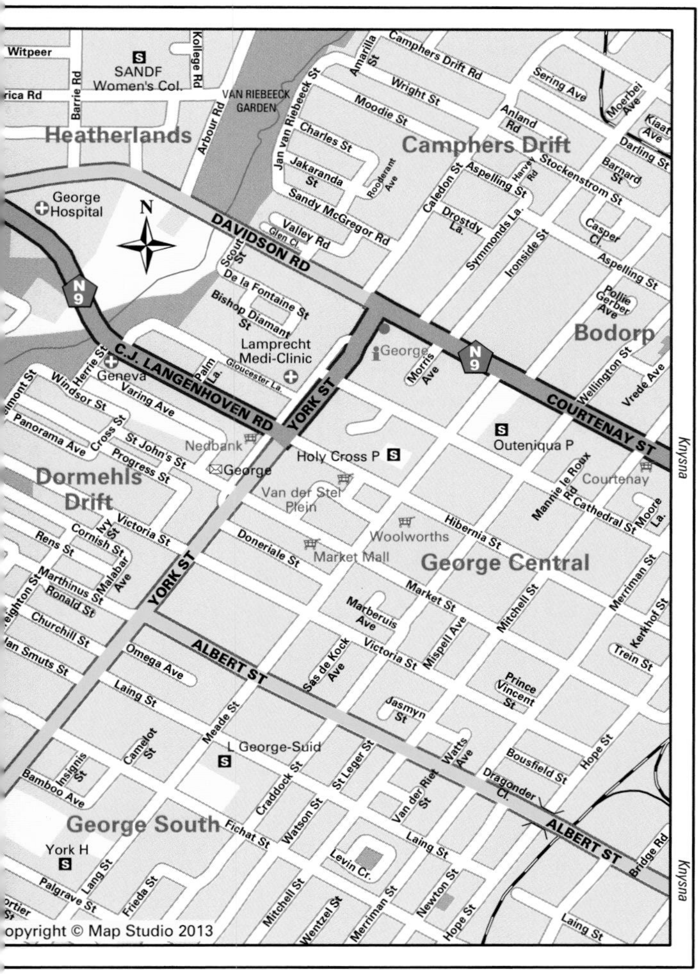

Wilderness

Port Elizabeth
Touws River
Milkwood Village
Wilderness
George

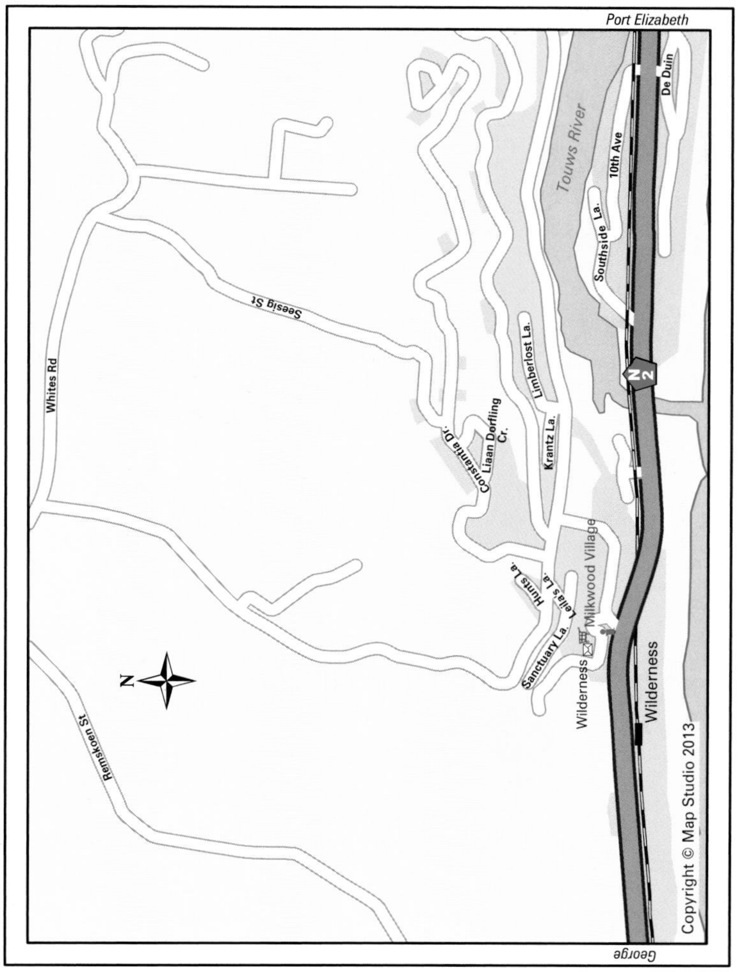

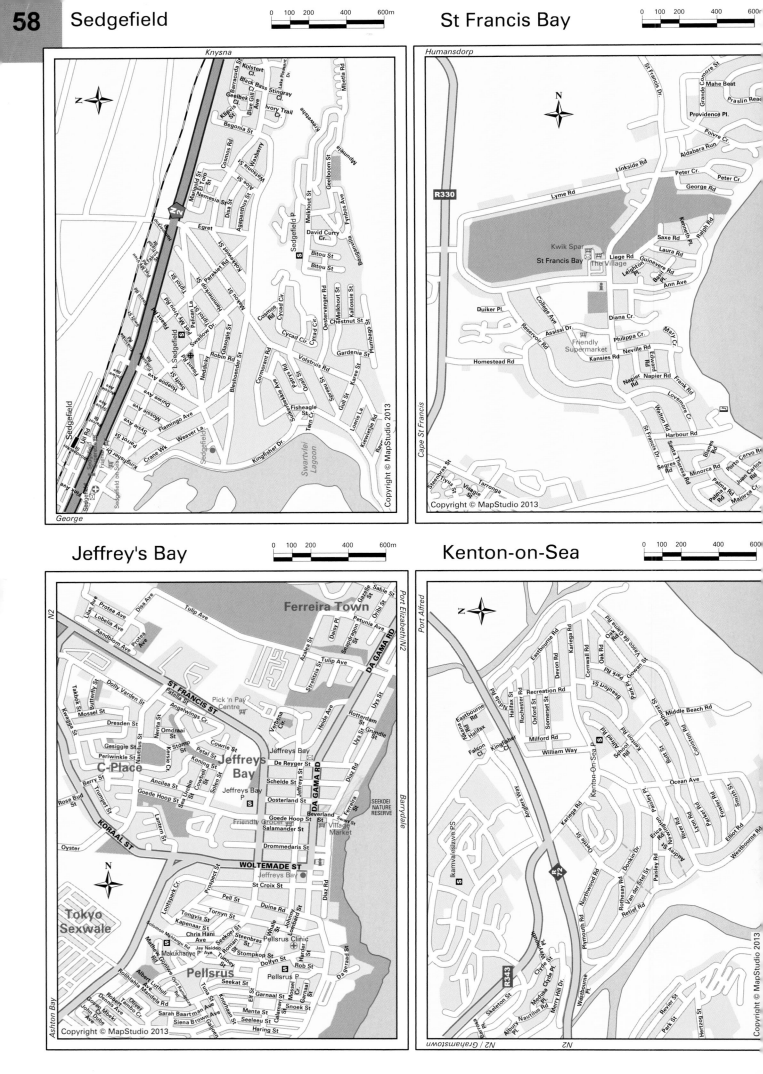

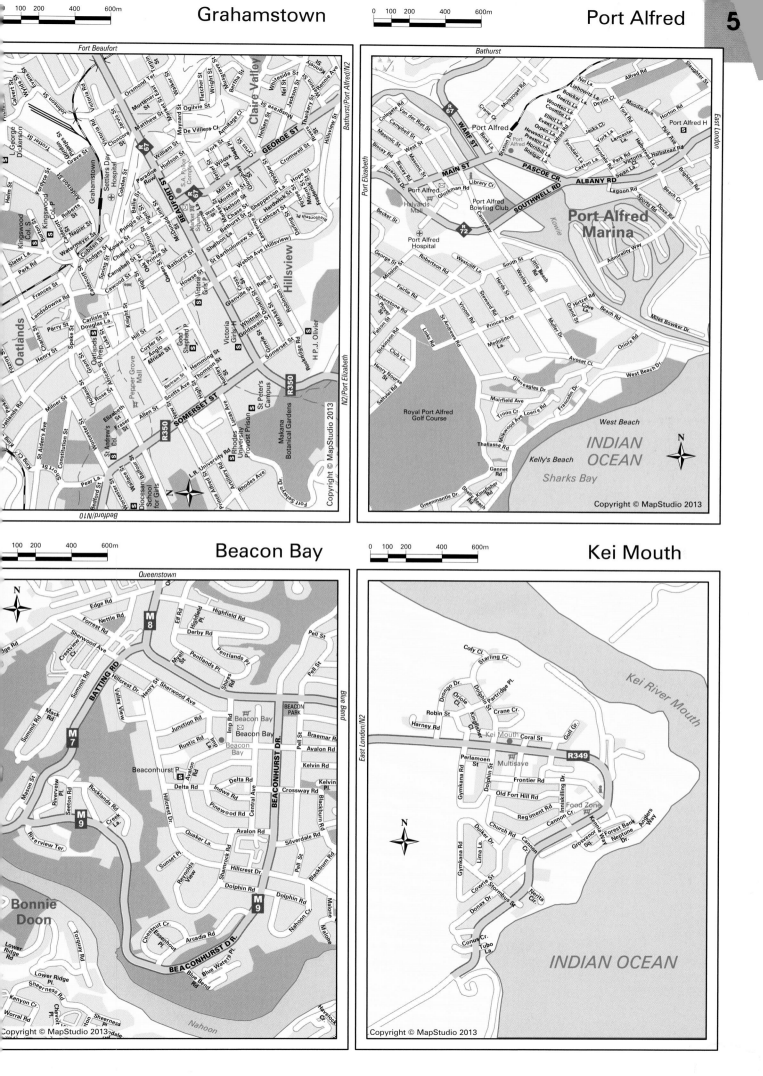

Index To Place Names

NO.	SOUTH	EAST	PG	GRID	NO.	SOUTH	EAST	PG	GRID	NO.	SOUTH	EAST	PG	GRID
J1	33°53'06.89"S	18°31'52.92"E	10	EJ 14	J49	33°35'57.01"S	22°11'53.04"E	25	EH 27	J97	32°34'50.64"S	25°08'16.79"E	43	ED 38
J2	34°20'58.25"S	18°28'59.97"E	10	EK 14	J50	33°31'58.09"S	21°41'19.33"E	25	EG 25	J98	32°07'53.87"S	25°31'21.99"E	43	EC 39
J3	34°09'39.86"S	19°01'58.74"E	11	EK 16	J51	33°49'09.52"S	22°21'16.45"E	26	EH 28	J99	32°10'08.90"S	25°37'01.18"E	44	EC 44
J4	34°13'52.85"S	19°11'17.33"E	11	EK 16	J52	33°29'39.93"S	22°31'58.38"E	26	EG 29	J100	31°39'03.10"S	25°48'34.03"E	44	EA 40
J5	34°13'38.40"S	19°25'44.76"E	11	EK 17	J53	33°18'23.50"S	22°28'29.26"E	26	EG 28	J101	32°39'53.82"S	25°53'05.85"E	44	ED 41
J6	34°21'06.73"S	19°39'47.15"E	11	EK 18	J54	33°39'28.42"S	23°07'15.38"E	27	EH 31	J102	32°00'27.05"S	26°15'31.87"E	44	EB 42
J7	34°26'24.52"S	19°27'34.32"E	11	EL 17	J55	33°30'14.51"S	23°13'31.68"E	27	EG 31	J103	32°22'19.89"S	26°55'25.11"E	45	EC 44
J8	34°05'16.94"S	20°05'26.17"E	12	EJ 20	J56	33°16'38.45"S	23°29'20.02"E	27	EG 32	J104	32°18'05.29"S	27°08'25.17"E	45	EC 45
J9	34°06'27.72"S	20°20'59.3"E	12	EJ 21	J57	33°36'08.14"S	24°12'05.28"E	28	EH 34	J105	31°53'35.30"S	26°52'27.20"E	45	EB 44
J10	34°31'56.51"S	20°02'29.49"E	12	EL 19	J58	33°39'32.15"S	24°31'55.35"E	28	EH 36	J106	32°33'57.46"S	27°25'02.08"E	46	ED 46
J11	34°22'25.19"S	20°23'30.09"E	12	EK 21	J59	33°19'48.26"S	24°20'39.95"E	28	EG 35	J107	31°31'23.37"S	27°41'41.38"E	46	EA 47
J12	34°06'41.16"S	20°56'05.95"E	13	EJ 23	J60	32°56'34.76"S	24°40'03.98"E	28	EE 36	J108	31°40'21.07"S	27°59'56.24"E	46	EA 48
J13	34°05'37.02"S	21°15'04.27"E	13	EJ 24	J61	33°05'38.07"S	24°52'09.96"E	29	EF 37	J109	32°00'11.44"S	27°46'43.84"E	46	EB 48
J14	34°10'09.48"S	21°19'16.98"E	13	EK 24	J62	33°17'45.08"S	24°49'54.06"E	29	EG 37	J110	32°34'47.53"S	27°57'09.54"E	46	ED 48
J15	34°18'37.91"S	21°01'48.48"E	13	EK 23	J63	33°26'20.21"S	25°16'25.82"E	29	EG 38	J111	32°19'04.58"S	28°10'08.01"E	47	EC 49
J16	34°12'01.35"S	21°40'38.15"E	14	EK 25	J64	33°45'23.91"S	25°24'25.97"E	29	EH 39	J112	32°38'09.57"S	28°25'37.61"E	47	ED 51
J17	34°11'02.59"S	22°07'23.63"E	14	EK 27	J65	33°36'43.84"S	25°54'49.89"E	30	EH 41	J113	32°05'43.36"S	28°18'04.33"E	47	EB 49
J18	33°59'07.37"S	22°30'32.68"E	15	EJ 29	J66	33°49'18.52"S	25°38'50.77"E	30	EH 40	J114	31°43'26.04"S	28°41'15.99"E	47	EA 51
J19	34°02'10.75"S	23°02'54.06"E	15	EJ 30	J67	33°26'11.10"S	25°57'45.79"E	30	EG 41	J115	31°35'18.03"S	28°47'24.22"E	47	EA 51
J20	34°02'29.31"S	23°06'16.42"E	16	EJ 31	J68	32°44'39.56"S	25°48'15.57"E	30	EE 40	J116	31°35'26.47"S	28°51'08.40"E	48	EA 52
J21	34°03'01.04"S	23°21'57.82"E	16	EJ 32	J69	32°43'01.40"S	25°35'11.34"E	30	EE 40	J117	31°37'32.02"S	29°32'36.29"E	48	EA 54
J22	33°59'56.89"S	24°14'09.08"E	17	EJ 35	J70	32°46'44.23"S	26°37'34.32"E	31	EE 43	J118	31°58'58.97"S	29°09'01.38"E	48	EB 53
J23	34°01'39.96"S	24°36'02.68"E	17	EJ 36	J71	33°11'57.68"S	27°07'05.97"E	31	EF 45	J119	31°57'47.31"S	23°45'49.61"E	41	EB 33
J24	34°07'10.77"S	24°53'30.17"E	18	EJ 37	J72	33°18'11.86"S	26°31'27.06"E	31	EG 43	J120	32°00'23.03"S	27°00'15.07"E	45	EB 45
J25	34°07'12.67"S	24°53'58.74"E	18	EJ 37	J73	33°35'55.46"S	26°53'27.2"E	31	EH 44					
J26	33°56'29.45"S	25°35'24.77"E	19	EJ 40	J74	32°52'43.24"S	27°23'46.63"E	32	EE 46					
J27	33°01'30.47"S	18°06'23.67"E	20	EF 12	J75	32°57'49.68"S	27°55'11.63"E	32	EE 48					
J28	32°54'17.18"S	17°59'23.43"E	20	EE 12	J76	32°41'03.88"S	28°22'29.19"E	33	EE 50					
J29	33°12'37.93"S	18°11'31.42"E	21	EG 13	J77	31°36'37.04"S	18°43'49.23"E	35	EA 15					
J30	33°49'52.91"S	18°32'21.98"E	21	EE 14	J78	31°46'49.03"S	18°37'57.96"E	35	EA 14					
J31	32°54'23.56"S	18°45'52.34"E	21	EE 15	J79	32°10'23.26"S	18°52'03.59"E	35	EC 15					
J32	33°09'06.22"S	18°39'58.67"E	21	EF 15	J80	32°21'50.38"S	18°56'21.46"E	35	EC 15					
J33	33°24'47.47"S	18°42'43.36"E	21	EG 15	J81	32°18'54.23"S	18°20'29.27"E	35	EC 13					
J34	33°27'41.77"S	18°43'22.31"E	21	EG 15	J82	32°16'32.22"S	19°13'01.43"E	36	EC 17					
J35	33°38'33.03"S	19°27'00.02"E	22	EH 17	J83	32°35'16.55"S	19°00'45.53"E	36	ED 16					
J36	33°30'55.01"S	19°11'23.71"E	22	EG 16	J84	32°09'12.19"S	20°02'50.56"E	37	EC 20					
J37	33°25'14.06"S	19°15'51.87"E	22	EG 17	J85	32°25'07.09"S	19°59'33.11"E	37	ED 19					
J38	33°18'09.13"S	19°03'18.28"E	22	EG 16	J86	31°54'45.08"S	20°13'45.88"E	37	EB 20					
J39	33°00'41.26"S	18°59'45.13"E	22	EF 16	J87	32°23'36.64"S	20°39'44.57"E	38	ED 22					
J40	33°13'28.34"S	20°34'54.32"E	23	EF 15	J88	31°54'57.53"S	21°30'46.68"E	39	EB 25					
J41	33°23'50.84"S	19°50'17.17"E	23	EG 13	J89	32°26'10.03"S	21°45'15.42"E	39	ED 26					
J42	33°19'41.44"S	20°01'54.85"E	23	EG 13	J90	32°22'35.01"S	22°31'37.07"E	40	EC 28					
J43	33°49'47.41"S	20°04'52.23"E	23	EH 14	J91	32°06'42.52"S	22°26'54.85"E	40	EC 28					
J44	33°11'37.26"S	20°51'42.06"E	24	EF 22	J92	31°53'04.81"S	23°05'00.19"E	41	EB 31					
J45	33°29'32.38"S	21°16'02.03"E	24	EG 24	J93	31°43'33.63"S	23°26'40.92"E	41	EA 32					
J46	33°35'21.45"S	21°10'54.89"E	24	EH 24	J94	32°28'34.04"S	24°03'44.27"E	42	ED 34					
J47	32°59'15.22"S	21°40'52.68"E	25	EF 25	J95	32°15'00.39"S	24°32'07.63"E	42	EC 36					
J48	33°23'30.32"S	22°06'27.31"E	25	EG 27	J96	31°54'45.76"S	24°45'47.62"E	43	EB 37					

Notes